RUNES

A Review of Poetry

memory

CB Follett and Susan Terris, Editors

WINTER SOLSTICE 2003

ARCTOS PRESS

RUNES, A Review of Poetry: Memory

ISBN 1-9657015-9-X
Library of Congress Control Number 2003113048
Library of Congress Cataloging in Publication Data
1. Poetry 2. Poetry on Mystery 3. Poetry -- 21st Century

Cover and book design by Jeremy Thornton

Front cover photograph *Arbor* © by Margaretta K. Mitchell
Back cover photograph *Memento Mori* © by Margaretta K. Mitchell
Inside artwork © by: Beth Cagle Burt, CB Follett, Margaretta K. Mitchell, Dorothy Porter, Jeremy Thornton, and Sandy Tresan

Special thanks to Duff Axsom, Amber Flora Thomas, Sophie Orgish, and Jake Orgish for volunteering time and energy to help us get RUNES out to our contributors and our subscribers.

ARCTOS PRESS
P.O. Box 401
Sausalito, CA 94966-0401
CB Follett: Publisher
Runes, A Review of Poetry e-mail: RunesRev@aol.com
http://members.aol.com/runes

Published and printed in the United States of America.

Preface

This is the third edition of *RUNES, A Review of Poetry*. In 2001 we started with the theme of "Gateway", moved on to "Mystery" in '02; and now we present "Memory." In this volume, we think you'll find many familiar, even comforting, memories and some so startling and original they'll make you sit up straight and say, "Whoa!"

As editors, we continue to be thrilled with the idea of presenting the 100 best poems we receive in a calendar year. That said, we had over 7000 poems to consider this year; and, yes, the two of us still read everything at least twice. (Our "staff" includes two poets and two young teenagers who volunteer to help us staple, stuff envelopes, and get *RUNES* into the mail.) And, yes, we still write a personal note to every poet who submits to us. (Those of you who forget to send the requested SASE get e-mail replies that are somewhat less personal.) We've said from the beginning that part of the impetus behind *RUNES* is to treat other poets as we'd like to be treated when we send out our own work. Primarily, this means showing respect both to the poets and to their work, whether we accept a poem or not.

What has happened that we didn't anticipate is that we are building a community of poets across the country and around the world. Our community numbers close to 275 now. We meet at conferences like the Associated Writing Programs (AWP). We look one another up as we travel. We correspond by e-mail, exchange poems, notify one another of good news, report on job possibilities and or promising fellowships. This spring alone five of our *RUNES* poets called and/or e-mailed to tell us they'd won first book competitions!

This year, for the first time, we received poems from all 50 states as well as 20 foreign countries. *RUNES '03* in its final form has poets from 28 states and 7 foreign countries. We find we love not only the states or countries each poet comes from; but we love their hometowns, too. It's not all Chicago, New York, Los Angeles, and San Francisco. Or Philadelphia. (For some reason, this was a big year for poets from Pennsylvania.) This year's *RUNES* has poets from places such as Wellfleet, Massachussetts; Kathmandu, Nepal; Norton, Ohio; Jones, Oklahoma; Ferndale, Michigan; Zwanenveld, The Netherlands; Mountain View, Arkansas; Burleson, Texas; and Haiku, Hawaii.

As a way of bringing this geographically diverse community together, we held a wine & cheese reception for all *RUNES* contributors, past and present, at AWP in Baltimore last year. We will do it again at AWP in Chicago in March. We also had *RUNES* readings in San Francisco, Los Angeles, Boston, New York, and St. Louis. We're certainly open to extending this to other cities in 2004. Philadelphia, here we come?

Whether a poet is from Philadelphia or Bala Cynwind, PA: we're crazy about the cover letters we receive. We love them, not for their impressive publishing credits, but because they give us a sense of who the poets are who submit to us. One volunteered to bake brownies for us if we'd accept a poem. Another offered a ride on his motorcycle (extra helmet included). A third suggested we have perfect names for poets (Follett? Terris? Hmm...) When we had winnowed the 7000 poems to those we absolutely couldn't live without, we had 300 poems in the **YES** category. That means we had to turn down 200 poems we really wanted to publish. So how, you ask, do we ever decide? Well... as editors, we like to be surprised. We *are* partial to the natural world, quirky information, and interesting titles (if the poem fulfills the promise of that title). Open this anthology and you can read, "My Mother Sends Wildwood to the First Grade," "Making Love at the Frost Place," "Car Advertising Alligator Farm," and "Love in the Time of Dioxin." (Of course, we also have poems with titles as simple as "Snake," "Silence," "Ring," and "Work.")

In this volume, there are poems in Russian, Spanish, Romanian, Hungarian, Tamil, and Ahtna Athabaskan; and if you don't read all of those languages, you'll find the translations on the facing pages. You will also find a stunning David St. John poem that was too wide to fit our format (yes, turn the book sideways, Reader.) We have intellectual poems, anti-intellectual poems, rhymed poems and free verse. gabrielle jesiolowsky wrote three drafts of an obituary for herself. We heard Corie Feiner recite "Tattoos" to warm up a slam competition in Baltimore and spent three days trying to find her so we could ask for the poem. Last year we seemed to have a lot of poems with dogs in them. This year: it's birds. Well, we like dogs and birds. There are more political poems in this *RUNES* than in the two past issues. War in Iraq, we think, plus post 9-11 concerns. And, of course, with a theme of "Memory" you'll find a good number of pieces about aging and and death issues as well as ones that reflect on the joyful and spiritual moments in a life. *RUNES* '03 has at least three poets who have never been published before, including our contest winner. Of the 100 poems in this issue, 81 are by poets we've never published before.

While we were enthusing about hometowns, we purposely withheld (suspense, suspense) the most important *RUNES* town for '03: *Mecca, California*! Yes, Mecca (how symbolically wonderful!) is the hometown of Mark Chapman, winner of this year's *RUNES* **Award** for his gorgeous poem "Farming Below Sea Level." We're thrilled that our judge Li-Young Lee selected Mark's poem and also the pieces by our two runners up: Lynne Knight and Kyoko Uchida. We congratulate all three of these poets, since their winning poems were selected from a pool of over 3000.

We hope you will search out these marvelous *RUNES* **Award** poems. At the same time, we'd like you to begin at the beginning and read straight through from cover to cover, since we've tried to make each poem speak in some way to the poem just before and just after it. This year, as many of you have requested, we've put our contributors' names on the back cover; but we still hope you'll read poems by poets you don't know as well as ones by poets with more familiar names. Part of being a community is continuing to expand horizons.

We hope we are continuing to expand ours, too. We love what we do. We are still amazed at the unsolicited praise the publication receives from all across the country, but that's not why we're involved in this venture. This is a labor of love. To be able to present *RUNES* to you is a privilege. We are fierce and proud, as parents are about a promising youngster, and also humbled by the sheer quality of the poems submitted to us and by the ones we've chosen for this volume. May you love *RUNES* '03 half as much as we do. Thank you for your enthusiasm and your support.

CB Follett & Susan Terris, Editors

TABLE OF CONTENTS

ARTWORK

CANDID CAMERA PHOTO SERVICE CO.

easure Island · · · San Francisco, California

DING POSTAGE GUARANTEED

1939

La Favorita—

CB Fallott

memory

The Blue Dogs of Scylla

caeruleis canibus resonantia saxa (Aeneid III)

As soon as I've left the reefs behind
and the thrashing straits, and when I've found
my sea legs, when I've caught the wind
and penned the flapping sails around it –
taken the whole wet shaggy air
and brought it to heel and got the waves
to lie down at my dry feet – then
I hear the yelping from the caves
behind me, where the rocks resound
again with the ocean-kennels' baying,
howling me back to them again
as if I'd never been away:
It's memory; it's back there, playing.
The sea-whelps leap in the grotto there –
the foam-white tongues and the old green claws
tear at my ankles with their spray
and take me back in their dark blue jaws.

Mnemosyne (Memory)

*Mnemosyne, according to Greek tradition, was
mother of the Muses, who inspired the arts of humankind*

Mnemosyne rises like a geyser from the hissing
spring; she calls her mourning daughters to her side –
the long-haired Muses, on whom the old bards
called when, taking lyre in hand, they gave
heroic measures to a dying world,
to war – a story and a musical score,
for brothers dead at each other's hands:
choral odes of praise –
Victory has come to Thebes!

In shamē, the Muses turn away, tend
only the wounded now, their once bright
garments filthy and torn; bits of glass,
shrapnel and bone in their hair, gray
with age, horror, the dust of mortar blown
from demolished rooms; exposed to air, the torn
mesh of deserted looms turn
to grimy cobwebs, catching bits of ash
and flesh; Memory's daughters
keen and tear their hair, while nearby,
drunken men piss into the ditch, then raise
the bucket from the local well to use
for target practice, and as the last of the water
dribbles through the holes – Amnesia,
dumb sister of Mnemosyne, brings her daughters
forward, offering them to the sons of men,

that they *long remember nothing
neither wind nor wake.*

After an Illustration by Rockwell Kent for *Moby Dick*, in Which a Whale Takes a Dory in its Maw, and Heads for the Bottom of the Sea

Through a night-sea, through krill,
chased down by stars.
The albacores scurry away.
An ocean, otherwise, so calm.
The spears are gone, the whaler's awl,
a bucket with which we might have bailed.

It was the middle of a marriage,
eight years before the break.
From Provincetown, we rode to the whales
aboard a watching-boat,
and from their pod, one rose along the rail –
barnacled, his breath so foul
I did not want to be consumed.
As if the legend might be true –
we could be swallowed alive, descend
to the sea grass and marl,
and live to tell of it.

Last week, this dream: waves
like an endless field, a battered dory,
the furious oars.
As the watching-boat turned,
I saw the whale rise – blue skin
breaking the surface, a vast swirl
of tail and the closure around it.
When I said *Look!* the whale was gone.
There was only the clatter of that engine,
and the wake, gun-metaled, churning upon itself.

Sea Memory

> The fish's soul
> is his empty bones.
> –Yehuda Amichai

On that shore – driftwood, empty bones bumping
      up against rocks, low-tide beneath
a lace-window sky, a ribbed articulation of clouds
      at the edges, sparing us nothing, as forecast,
in the way of regret. We would lie then along the cloud-
      grey sand, in our unconscious youth, in the cool,
overhanging leaf shade bruises of the eucalyptus,
      and let our eyes fill with the watery apparatus
of a washed-out and abstract blue, day-dreaming
      through the daffodil light of Judy Holliday
in "Bells Are Ringing" or Sandra Dee in "A Summer Place."
      We didn't have the first idea about ideas,
and, diving under kelp beds, shot the carefree fish
      with our hand-sling spears and never gave
a thought to what the trident symbolized – the soul
      was only something in a catechism text,
an emptiness in the air we were never going to touch,
      unlike the eucharist-white bones of the fish.
And when the only bass I ever speared wriggled
      on the tines of the bright and awful air,

the slash its side unfolded like bread soaked in wine,
  and its amber eye beheld me there and all the sky
could see who I was and had become with its ichor
  oozing on my sea-stained hands. And still
what sweet language the plovers and godwits sent up
  despite me in my frogman flippers and mask
that disguised so little as I thrust my stick and defied
  next to nothing in the sky. The gulls praised
the flesh of the world, and flew their grey rags of death,
  and loitered on the logs and seaweed there –
patient again as death – to see what I would do. And though
  wave after wave testified against me, I knew
no sorrow, and felt innocent as sea foam, unassailed
  as the blue-roofed bungalows of the resort,
the weekenders on the boardwalk, the ice plant
  over the seawall and the dunes. Everything
was, for the most part, unknown – the ridicule of the wind,
  the resurrection of dust, my spindrift breath,
and the ocean's churning roots – just driftwood bumping,
  beached forever – the sea wrack of the heart.

Cullet

Ugly fish of a word   for the hardened beauty   blown neck
   of what gets thrown away   refused.
      Then taken up in a pocket   given away. Treasured
         in a velvet drawstring pouch. Utterly useless. Like memory.
      Memory's fixative.   Scrap.   Discard. Black
   as some waters (though not Venice's canals).
Fat bauble   headless
   fertility goddess   gold paint
      drizzled diagonal
         down one side. Rough
      spot to the touch could even cut skin
   where it was twisted off in fire.
Heavy in the hand
   and in the pocket to carry as the German father on the local vaporetto
      must have felt watching his young daughter
         befriended by a mother and son in English making a bridge
      of chatter all the way from the Rialto to the Giardino where we parted
   in search of a child's swing.
Reflective enough to see (did I mention?)
   the lamp lighting my peering in so that writing this
      I stand outside and within. Recall his smile,
            hand in pocket, composing something:
      loquacious American mother and child – his Venetian tale –
   just as he and the girl
and the broken-off piece he gave us – ours.

The Shortcut Home

In my sister's story,
my mother swears we were born,
but God can't find us
in any of his coat pockets,
not in the empty, and not in the filled.
We're in none of his hands, the fine or the terrible,
none of his shoes, the giant or the minute.
And neither are we hiding inside his apples,
neither the perfect nor the ruined.
Not in the first mouthful, and not in the last.

In my brother's story,
our death sings to us from the highest branch
of the oldest tree the birds remember
in song, and we wander our father's house
in search of the origin of the hours.

In my story… But I don't have a story.
All I have a few few names of the flowers:
Morning Glory, Seven O'Clock, Mother of Wings,
Dreaming Undone, Dreaming Shouldered,
Story Carried Backward Up a Stairs. All I have
is a sown path I follow back to sleep:
Painted Face, Clouded Pane, Song in a Jar,
Burning Threshold, Bloody Scrimmage,
Voice Strewn on the Rocks.

Female Scarecrow

The skirts flap in the garden,
        that worn cotton upon which
roses were printed

long ago
and have faded now, further back
than background, yet arc they not

more substantive
than the real remembered ones? – those blooming

in the vanished hedgerow –

and still, however pale, visible
unlike your mother living in the house
years ago, years

even before you arrived – little tangle
        of worry – already
too late.

And tell me, what should it
be frightening now? The barn
sails into evening,

the trees go, the road

and waves of deer
come from the woods up to the edge
of the garden. They walk,

all night, past the figure
that continues – not breathing –

but hanging there.

First Trip to the Infinite

Years before poptops, I held a can of orange soda
and looked through the triangle my mother's church key made.
I was five or six, next to my brother on a redwood bench
in our backyard, and thought the spot of sun inside was a sailboat.
I loved the traversing reflections, the zippity gleam,
an enchanted door. I think I willed myself to become abstract –
(though I didn't know what that meant, it was the only way to enter –)
I moved the can from angle to angle, followed the gold parallelogram
and again the triangle – I crawled inside that vessel and traveled
from one orange shore to another, flew further and farther
to a region where light teemed forever
like the place where the fireflies we chased at dusk
were born. My eye on the flashes, little armadas
that couldn't sink in the ocean inside the aluminum walls
of the new world, I saw it was endless –
Not like the clothesline where my mother stretched her freckled arms.
Not like the games the other kids played till the sky went amethyst
and their houses called from the mouths of their doors. In the flickering
sloop of the can, I abandoned my brother, forgot
my lavender sunsuit, my bare feet and braided hair.
For one long moment I coasted
in the journeying bardo – lay down
in the curvature of the infinite
lit from within
like an orange is – circular, globular, spinning
to nothing, nothing
but center.

My Mother Sends Wild Wood to the First Grade

What obscure urge led her to it –
to dispatch such savage
luxuriance to show and tell.
The other kids brought
Betsy Wetsys or Davey
Crockett hats, or occasional
platesful of peanut butter cookies –
but to pile idolatrous armfuls
of Hera's apple
into the old Dodge, scandalous
scent of blossom clinging
to rolled upholstery?

What could she have meant
by so extravagant a gesture,
my middle-aged mother
in her stiff shirt waist
and sensible pumps?

I trudged somber corridors of
Sherman Elementary, beleaguered
with hieratic armfuls of blossom:
clouds of cherry, sprays of
apple, hot with steamy pollens
and the furred memories of bees.

Mrs. Nelson glared,
her red-powdered face ablaze,
at such unpunctuated abundance
let loose among the orderly rows
of desks, scent breaking,
like a an undisciplined child,
into the advanced reading circle.

I felt the heat rise up the backs of
my hands, the cords in my neck.
Who was this prim nyloned mother of mine?
How could she send me to this methodical place,
where paper tulips precisely lined
beige bulletin boards and chalk trays
held clapped erasers, where
the thin white dust of
industry settled over everything
and paper was neatly ruled, how could she
send me here, smelling
of the opulent, naked skin
of trees.

a theory of snow

then, the winter you were eight the sharp
arguments of the world digressed
into an unrelenting, undressing dream of snow
flake by flake the ashen sky fell to a thronging hush
piled up at the bottom frames of doors
as if to add to each mute mouth a perfect lip

from the front window you observe
the hunched white bulk of cars
staggered like blind beasts wandered from their stalls
stilled full speed in your childhood
you watch white hold   the way white in a painting does
or wind a sail

see for yourself in the row of muffled houses
the fugitive nature of what slides beneath a name
before even the purple stripes behind trees appear
you know a loneliness that will not change
a place rooted in you   bitter and serene   something final
like a clearing of the land   or a black pond filling to the brim

Stoppered Heart Blessing #9

Sidewalks coming back out of ice   two of us under
bare maple trees   our boot-marks in the snow-mush by the school-bus
stop   dark bird we have forgotten   the fight that sent me home
long bloody scratches   hank of her hair in my hand
we are talking about   the snow bowl made this morning   left
in deep shade under cypress   by our cave underneath the front porch
i can tell her anything now   anything   so i tell her the bowl
is our future   as long as it lasts the earth will be safe   when it melts
we will die   and she believes me   she really believes me   icicle-
melt on our jackets   we climb the steps of the bus   push toward
the cracked leather seats we prefer   don't worry i say
we will go on   as long as the snow bowl is there we are safe
cold dirty shadowed   hunkered down among trees
the world will be held

I Return to Fayetteville After Twenty Years

Four starlings bathe in a pothole, dipping
and shivering. The Methodist Church chimes
electric hymns – same town, but brightened,
wide-eyed, no nostalgia to hide in.
A high-rise apartment for seniors has been
superimposed on the old Junior High,
and so on.
            Me, I'm sitting in detention hall
in Junior High, desks bolted to the floor.
 I've grown so tall, though, that I hover
over myself, where I am scratching a crude house
on the desk top with a straightened paper clip.
I lean down as if life is a lesson I have to teach.
Look! I say to myself, that's you in the house,
crumbling shredded wheat in the bowl.
There's your mother, so alive the hairs on her arm
glisten. There are the chimes, and the space
between hymns where this other can get in.

Love in the Time of Dioxin

the girl steps into the tattoo parlor
'truth' is on her body: trysts

now nameless
pain of ink

etched into skin: *forever*
she thinks, *I will not betray*

word from the past

a Japanese calligraph
between ribs & breasts

*

pain is a reflection
aftermath

– this is not it
& out the door

for a moment's pleasure
this is not it

body-scar
the ink reminder

Ceiling

As a kid, I used to pretend
        to walk on the ceilings of my parents' house;
    I'd hold a mirror like a plate, or a tray,
the way I'd use it later

to snort a line of coke off of –
        but before I discovered more sophisticated ways
    of making the world disappear,
I'd go from room to room

looking down into the mirror,
        stepping carefully over doorjambs
    and around light fixtures,
happy as the flies that crawled up there,

or as happy as I imagined flies
        must be, though really who knew about them,
    they always sounded so angry
with their tiny buzzsaw voices –

In the real house, my brother
        would be trying to slam my father into a doorway
    or chasing his siblings
around the table with a butcher knife;

he'd pull me out of hiding in a closet
   to practice hitting something weaker. No wonder
  I wanted to live on the pure white ceiling
and inhale the clean granules that turned

my brain starry, no wonder I envied
   the flies, caroming above us, or tracking through sugar
  and careening out the open screen door
though sometimes someone picked up a swatter

and smacked them dead against
   the window glass – a fate I also occasionally envied –
  but now I'm glad I'm here,
years and miles from my handsome, troubled family,

on vacation next to a shimmering lagoon
   with egrets wading into their serene reflections
  and workmen on the roof next door
hammering and sawing, the sound of repair going on all day.

Negligee, Negligence, Negligent

Here, sidling up to the house where she was raised, the rooms aglow with ghosts,
daytime ghosts in cahoots with the sunshine, panes unable to hold a single thing
back: her father, squinting at a verse, her mother, licking stamps.

Nothing here was a waste of time.
Nothing crept so slowly.

Here, the slender neck of Nefertiti rises in limestone from the photographs,
   All this fiddle, the ears begin to say,
   Beyond, the eyebrows say,
   Nothing nefarious, from the slender shoulders, *as your own heart*.

What in history would you call your own?

She curls against the brick as best she can, the simple girl,
giving her body to the hard wall of memory, the topography of this place
home: once she saw a peregrine falcon, heard a hundred pond frogs.

And wouldn't you know a girl is only a scrap of soft fabric with legs,
   walking backwards toward love,
   strolling sideways toward love,
   fluttering across the waters in her way.

She turns. For all your permanent shimmer, the cloth of my skin
is young, is questing, dilapidated with chance.
Something, O Queen, knows me better than I know myself.

God shaped the fields of sorghum just so?

Memory

hard eraser's grit
and crumble.

*

Memory

her red shirt tucked
in, she leaned out, her lips
poised for a kiss
over the cliff
        sadly
she buttoned the top
of her jeans and left,
sadly–imagined wave,
gentle wake.

*

Memory

yellowed names on a list
broken rotary dial
snowflake moon
nobody rising
from the dead.

*

Memory

Flicker.
Then silence,
or steady hum.

Letters to Juliet

When Barbara calls from Verona, she says
they're looking for a woman to answer
                all the letters addressed to Juliet Capulet,
because the woman who's answered them for years
        is tired of the *problemi di cuore* and wants to retire.
Problems of the heart: these, at least, haven't changed.

        In the Dark Ages of my own life,
I had fantasies of myself as a swashbuckler,
                stuffing my pouch with the gems I'd sucked
from the navels of dusky maidens,
        though my search for amorous adventures
just led me into one utterly inappropriate relationship

        after another, such as the one with the woman
who claimed she could make people disappear completely
                except for their eyes. And that's love, sure,
though love's also Pepi Deutsch hoarding three slices
        of bread and slathering them with marmalade
so she can make her daughter Clara

        a 17th-birthday cake in the hell of Auschwitz-Birkenau.
And it's 50-year-old Antonio Delfini opening the bier
                of his father, who had died when he was 30, and weeping
as he gazes at the body of a man 20 years younger than himself.
        Now who was he loving, his father or himself?
Surely both, for while we love those we love

almost with all our hearts, we love ourselves even more,
which means we pity ourselves even more,
                    as I do now, for instance, because while I'm grateful
for the silence in which to read and write for hours on end,
          I can't help thinking, from time to time, that one day
this room will be forever silent except for the sound of one person

          making coffee or pressing the collar of an old shirt,
and that person could be either of us –
                    unless one day we're in our eighties, say, on a flight to,
oh, I don't know, Prague, and we have a couple of icy martinis
          on the tray tables in front of us, and one seat over,
this nervous guy opens his carry-on bag, and inside it there's this bomb. . . .

          Maybe all love is self-love.
Maybe, when the *New York Times* food critic said the best Wiener schnitzel
                    he ever had wasn't all that much different from
the worst Wiener schnitzel he ever had,
          he meant that, taken as individuals, we are all too much
like Wiener schnitzel – too schnitzel-y, in a word.

          Last night, as I sat in the piazza, I thought of Barbara,
and as people opened and closed their shutters and lighted up
                    this room and darkened that one, I pretended
all the little flashes were the eyes of those who had disappeared
          and who'd come back to look for someone,
though who it was, they couldn't remember.

All Night, All Night, All Morning

No routine compensates for this dumb hour, the pane streaked and all
    manner of intransigence

Poised, ready to commit at day. I fold my hands and wait for the
    reconnaissance, its green twig, flesh

Against claw in defiance of gravity, wanting to feel that lightness
    lacing and unlacing,

Exchanging the orthogonal for the parallel. Fidelity mothers a good
    deal else

Besides ritual stutter, the page's analogue to its own break: implying
    a motion: a propulsive vector

Traveling on forged papers. The border drops away, childhood
    flensed in the glare of a bare bulb.

You said if I'd strip back the layers I'd become emperor
    over a fluid kingdom –

You promised me that buoyancy. Now my hands are cranes in the first
    light, fine-boned for a man's,

Astonished. Iridescent. Let need be our covenant in common salt,
    after the mercy's gone.

Making Love at the Frost Place

Franconia, NH

His name – **R. Frost** – writ large in bold strokes on the mailbox,
the village luminary
hunkers in wraithlike presence over his writing desk,
or shuffles in slippers past
the open hearth, milky hair and graphite-needled face
such familiar portraiture
we can't not see him rage as we clutch each other, not
hear him groan as we commence
late August lovemaking during such perishable
tenancy, until we learn
again, *night falling fast*, what schoolchildren flame to know:
the common language that breathes
autumn into *apples*, winter into *sleep* and *snow*.

Plasa de Apa

When the silent woman comes and beheads the tulips:
Who wins?
Who loses?
Who stands by the window?
Who'll be the first to say her name?
    —Paul Celan, "Chanson of a Woman in Shadow"

Aşa cum eu după atâţia ani
nu mă pot desprinde de imaginea noastră
(înotător tânăr ieşind din ape
călăuzit de lumina apusului
undeva, pe malul fluviului,
şi eu aşteptându-te pe ţărm,
jucându-ne apoi jocul unei morţi surâzătoare
şi simplitatea, mai ales simplitatea
acelui salt în mijlocul elementelor)
astfel şi tu
ar trebui să mă urăşti mai puţin
pentru tot ceea ce nu s-a mai întâmplat
niciodată la fel.
Să-ţi aminteşti doar plasa de ierburi şi apă
şi înotătorii acelui apus
în mijlocul,
în groapa,
în ochiul crăpat o clipă de moartea
la care încă nu se gândeau.

The Web of Water

When the silent woman comes and beheads the tulips:
Who wins?
   Who loses?
      Who stands by the window?
Who'll be the first to say her name?
         —Paul Celan, "Chanson of a Woman in Shadow"

Just as, years later,
I can't let go of our image
(a young swimmer stepping from the water
to the riverbank
guided by the last glow of sunset,
I waiting for you on the shore,
then our play, the game of grinning death,
and the simplicity, above all the simplicity
of that dive, into the heart of the elements),
so you in turn
shouldn't hate me so much
for everything that could never happen
the exact same way again.
Remember only the web of weeds and water,
the swimmers in the heart
of sunset,
in the grave,
in the eye barely opened for an instant by death,
to which as yet they give no thought.

his poem (without adjectives)   her blues

his poem (without adjectives)	her blues
For a year	– and the teaspoons
we had nothing	you gave me
but anniversaries	are tadpoles running
of events	through my fingers
we pieced together	in dishwater, oh
from letters	not really –
and photos,	unless
albums of night-	the traffic
and daymares.	on Race St. is
It was the season,	a multi-colored chain,
a summer without	or a pigeon flock
warmth, like you said	is scattered cards
on the solstice:	winging their numbers
"After this	away, or
the year chills	a car door
into January..."	screeling open
and the radio played	in icy wind
"*Nothing changes*	is a seagull
on New Year's Day"	crying over the lot –
– nothing except	and who is
loyalties,	facing me
addresses,	and always was

friends, jobs, and
everyone's in
Berlin or Trieste
or Paris, even
Bangladesh,
whereas I
journeyed by
standing in place,
watched a world
drift under the snow –
It's just like this,
when you have
a year of
anniversaries,
a year without
  a   memory –
  each word
   exhales
into   fog
   as if it
were whited out.

comes through me,
a melody
luring me in
like a velvet dress
or a dark pond
that injures me –
and I never
hear over three-
thousand miles
that you're some-
where else till I read
"Itemized Calls" like
breaking china –
even if
I stop dancing,
even if
I start
laughing
at photos
of accidents
in the papers.

Ring

In the beginning it was like fire.
And in the end.
He slipped the ring from his finger.
No, slipped
is not true. It was more difficult, more
painful. It hurt to twist
and pull the ring
from his finger. And then

there was a ring
on the table. A silver thing
on white cloth. A circle, or a zero,
a halo of knowing.
A creeping burn
around the pinkened flesh
where the ring
had been for years. A memory.
A sting.

Debt Of Gratitude

They say it is a love story. I do not
deny it. She arrives in snow falling fast as any
longing, in white like a ghost or a bride.
In the folktale I remember, it is an old woman who
takes her in, whose husband once took pity on a crane.
Who else but a poor childless couple to be blessed
with a daughter and unending bolts of purest white silk,
rich as the moonlight she weaves by?

They say no, it is a young hunter instead, dumbstruck
and eligible, whose kindness she's come to repay.
At her loom each night she hides her feathered self
so that she might stay his wife, out of love. And it is
out of desire for her pale smooth neck that he breaks
his promise not to look. There is no other explanation.

In my version, by winter's end the old woman sees,
as only a mother would, that her daughter grows thin
with every thread. This is why she looks:
Every mother believes she has the right to know.
In the morning the crane must leave, weeping at the woman's
betrayal. It's as if all this time she'd been weaving
her own funeral shroud.

Or wedding dress. My mother says, *It's about time*.
Even in this children's tale of virtue and debt of gratitude,
a girl must weep for her husband, not her mother.
They tell me that I should have known all along.

They say it is a love story. I do not
deny it: a love so necessary that in the end
we must turn even our daughters out.

A Mnemonic Device for Past Loves and the Sestina

Who was the spring to bring me one?
I would reach her by bicycle, two
wheels turning through the morning, the abandoned three-
wheeled yellow Bug in the drive, the sixty-four
Mustang on the curb, black. In my back pocket, five
poems about five nights. I never wrote the sixth.

Some fall at first sight, others at the sixth;
after I heard her "r" trilling tongue, I hoped one
day my Anglo mouth would learn its grace. In our five
months, we were vaguely naked only twice
and never at the same time, but once, after four
tequila shots, I licked lime off her neck till three.

Time was dead by the open blue of her eyes, three
kisses lasted an afternoon, and that night, on the sixth
green, I wriggled her jeans down enough to touch, for
luck, her humid and haired mouth. Pleasure? One
of us would not forget. Later, two
thousand miles apart, we loved by phone after five.

This one sucked my ear, hard, while going 95
on I-5 south to north L.A. She tried three
times to take what I wanted to lose, but had to wait two
months and break up once before consummation at six
on her futon, or in the mouth of night in the hall, or once,
at noon, lakeside. I still hate who she left me for.

Some loves come by pure voice, like those four
elegies of Rilke's or the open way all five
of our senses gave in to us. My nose was one
for the geranium of her curled dark hair. Three
of her fingers stroked my temple at dawn while six
bird cries rang through. Daughter of kings, where have you gone to?

All the gratuitous countries conspired to
give us a second chance. She left Florence and four
lovers there, I was fresh back from Nepal and six
weeks in a monastery. At five
o'clock in the fall, we met again; three
hours later, our shadows were on the wall as one.

When dead, one thing must be said at my $2
funeral attended by three crows: "Spit out your quartet
of lies about love and seek all five tastes in one mouth, or six."

Tünemény

Füstszinu falusi alkonyat vagy.
Mosolyod illatos kenyerét tétován
tördeli az emlékezés.

Hol volt, hol nem volt, volt egy lány...
Hiába próbálok neveket
illeszteni a mosolyodhoz.

Egy fehér-homlokú házra s egy lombos
eperfára emlékszem,
s hogy jött a csorda.
Ránk bámult egy bivaly. – Mozgás, Rigó! –
Húzott rá a napszitta pásztor.
És Rigó unottan tovább kolompolt.
Hangoltak a békák a libaúsztatóban;
holdat himbált a szello a domb fölé észrevétlen.
Zizegett a nád.
Mindenre emlékszem, úgy-ahogy,
– talán még azt a zsombékot is meglelném –
csak rád, az arcodra, a mozdulataidra – nem.
Vagy nem is voltál más,
csak egy soha-el-nem-felejtheto mosoly,
mely minden nyári alkonyatkor
a langyos szellovel s a füst illatával
meg-megkisérti emlékezetem? –
Néha már-már látlak, érzem, amint hajad
ujjaim közé omlik, mint akkor.
De hiába, valami mindig eloroz elolem,
és alkonyatból alkonyatba menekit.

Mirage

Smoke-colored village dusk, that's you.
Remembrance testingly kneads
the fragrant bread of your smile.

Once upon a time there was a girl...
It's no use trying to fit
a name into the story.

I remember a cottage with a whitewashed forehead,
the full foliage of a mulberry tree,
and the herd coming home from the pasture.
An ox stopped to stare at us. – Move on, Rigo! –
there was a whack from the cowherd.
And Rigo's bell started to ring again.
The frogs were tuning up in the goose pond;
the breeze was swinging the moon over the hill.
There was a hiss in the sedge.
I can remember it all, or just about all,
– I might even find the hillock in the marsh –
it's only you, your face, your gestures that elude me.
Or else, you were nothing but
a never-to-be-forgotten smile
that tickles my memory
at every summer twilight
with smoke-flavored breeze.
Sometimes I can see you and feel your hair
cascading between my fingers as back then.
But it's no use, you've been abducted from me
and made to flee from one dusk to the next.

Home after Holidays

In that living room someone will be telling someone
               of old transgressions, intoning them habitually
     as the cavity filled by an internal organ.

How do the lips form them?
     Such flattened words
          and still pressing?

They are not words. They are the shadows along the hall floorboards
               late at night after the children are in bed.

Street rain glazes black on the runway,
     black on the mailbox – this curb, this sign, this tree

understand, simultaneously, immersion.

While we're in our beds it will freeze
          and in the morning, if only you could
       find a prying point,

you could lift the ice relief off the town, whole.

Blind Mask

> Always arriving, you will go everywhere.
> –Rimbaud

Too fast to know
Where you are going,
To hear it arriving by mouth, messenger.
Like memory.
Adrenaline draws your blood's tin rust & taste from your mouth
On the fast track to nowhere, skimming whitecaps of clouds
And the drunken blue edge adjusting the sky
Your pulse taken from you
Like bones from their grave
The infinite story of light producing its own offspring
Dead man's float down the rapids
Double helix and wheel of recklessness
Intercourse with the 21st century way of life
But you must go anyway because

On your mark, you will never have to look back.
Get set for the next Thailand and Milan.
Go like the arrow you can't hear in the dark.
Go like fuck between first and second.
Go all the way down to the Grand Canyon bottom, bearing fossils
And a feel for dry air, leading with your jaw bone and your desire
To Go, Go...
Arrive highwire, with all your might and will to be the one
Checking out of the Emergency Room
Hidden from view
With your fake passport in one hand, and your next
Destination mapped on the other.

The Game Lords

They are the immortal renewers of substance –
the force behind and above animate nature.
                    –Loren Eiseley, "The Dance of the Frogs"

1. LABRADOR

Winter, and the Naskapi hide
under caribou skins and read signs
in the bones of eaten bear. From inside
their tents, they pray to the game lords,
spirits that awaken when the cold breaks
with spring, wet with the songs of frogs.

Their tents shake, their voices unite
with the frog chants, an invocation
for the pounding of hooves, for fish
or fur. They are not silent until morning.

2. PENNSYLVANIA

Lanterns pour their pale light
across a wharf, half-built
over a marsh that swells and sings
with frogs luring their mates.

A lone scientist counts the trills,
measures tones and grunts,
uses his instruments to tap
the mysteries of Naskapi lore.

Curiosity pulls him to the wharf
where his shadow spawns a line of men
alongside him, bounding heel-toe,
heel-toe from one lantern to the next.

He hears the frogs through the mist,
a chorus of trills called by the water.
Their shadows leer up beside him, giants
leaping to the pulse of the night in the wild
wetness of spring, their rhythm driving him
to leap, to keep pace, his shadow changing –
a half-man charging into the cacophony
of the swamp to become one of them –
until the terror that is alone human calls
out to the light on the wharf, shattering
the frenzy into silence.

3.   THE EXPLORERS CLUB

A brandy, a cheery fire, chats here
and there of travels and studies,
but he keeps to himself, remembering
that instant between desire and fear,
between the sacred shape of history
and the final leap into darkness,
that instant when knowledge falls
away like cracked teeth.

It is the question of choice, he says,
his batrachian hand hidden in a black glove –
the only proof.

He knows why the Naskapi read
their dreams in bones and wait
for the welcome hush of winter.

Like Tiny Bones Of The Feet

birds in sky

        personal realm   symbol   color   language

        hibernating   maps have voices
        point me toward   still arrows
          chalice with two eyes
                      (the animal awaits naming)

    without seasons   *which is to say*
        phosphorescence   unreleased memory

       the larger moves   when the small beckons

        power of tiny bones

         In dreams only one realm   mechanics of anatomy/
             geometry   tangle and untangle what I hear

upon waking

    some things which float   are really heavy

    some movements lie beyond physics

why is it so difficult for my hand to reach yours

Retribution

spread on the dirt like rice paper fans
    each a flawless design
of aerodynamic perfection

    the wings of birds

hunters leave them behind

    though severed, not aged
imprinted with memory of flight
    they were never meant to be so still

cats ignore them because they think
    without heads they are nothing

somewhere there are ghosts of birds
searching for wings
haunting men while they sleep
the men who hunted birds
and left their wings behind

Foxes

She wrote of foxes, small and densely furred,
dark forests where a girl might go to dream
and name her longings more than what they seem,
a promise shaped by just the perfect word.
Their tails were plumed; the stories that occurred
ran red with motion like an autumn stream
beyond what facts' sharp actions can redeem:
creative lying, deeper than what's heard.
And what of teeth? Hard eyes that shine and stare
with hollowed hunger winter thickens fast?
Small bony paws that reach out sure to dare
the shape of snow's own future, present, past?
She wrote of foxes: it's on us they feed,
the ones who need them, quickened as we read.

Owl Pellet

This owl, like me, likes to look back.
Unlike my rigid person, he
Can swivel his furred ear, his black
And golden eye to hear, to see,
Almost halfway round. He hunches,
Quasimodo, shrugs one slight shrug,
Then coughs remnants of his lunches
Where leafmold serves him as a rug.
No drunk's vomit this, no foul spew,
His dry retchings have been rounded,
Measured, parcelled, packed, reduced to
Pellets filled with what confounded
And dismayed his gut. I can find
Within the discards, souvenirs
Of what had filled his maw and mind
These nights: some tiny skulls whose fears
Hadn't kept their erstwhile owners
Home...polished vertebrae...legbones...
Gifts from small reluctant donors,
Gifts this sleepy owl treats as loans.
Old hours fill me too until at last
I, like this drowsy owl, disgorge the past.

Goldmund Unfettered

The animals in the lemon grove
have resigned themselves

in the event of another
flood of darkness

       to a long life
of dying off. Luna moths

   *   *   *   *

pulled into the slipstream
of the blue heating fan,

       for instance, spew their silver dust
over the backs and shoulders

of the laborers who prune the trees.
Fireflies touch down in a little crux

   *   *   *   *

the root of a cypress makes –
(as it wends its way

       around a stone) –
and in small piles

their sparks go out slowly
like sponges drying in the night.

   *   *   *   *

The mammals lie down
Wherever the urge strikes them,

stones of fur
on a lake of grass.

And who could forget
the humans?–that laborer with dark hair

*   *   *   *

        who sips a rose hip tea
and thirsts for new machines

as the lazy raven
opens his iridescent wing

        and blackens half the moon.
No more intermissions

*   *   *   *

for the scythe, no more
reprieves for the abandoned mill –

        who dreams
from deep within her rust

that given the right dose of faith
she might yet become a violin.

Horse

Carol lifted a skull out of the spring growth and took it home,
away from the field it called home. The skull was the house
she grew up in, the garden wild with rabbits, the fence
tufted with dog fur. The skull was her father's crown beneath

his thinning hair, him lifting her skirt. It was her spine, stiff
as a garden hose in winter. Carol placed the trophy above
her door by its sword nose. Horse might as well have been
swinging from oak like a criminal, far away from purple clover,

the miner's lettuce crowding the brook. Horse lifted its head
into the living space it no longer held and raged on the nail.
The sound rippled through the field of thistles,
spines erect as they waited for the crush of hoof.

Horse ached to lose the door, but frame would not let go.
Nail loosened like horse's teeth, but wood would not let go.
The dog whined at horse's invisible body as it kicked free.
Inside, horse's tail switched cobwebs loose and the dog nipped

at its flanks, but horse entered Carol's room and gnawed on her fingers.
Carol tried to find sugar in dream, sweet green apples. But horse,
wanting spring's growth in its nostrils, would not let up until Carol
gave in, her body coiling like a snake as she galloped it home to rest.

The Snake

Each morning I saw the dead snake on my path
down the two-track through the hardwoods.
When it was freshly killed it kept its roundness
still and the wet sheen of a brown whiteness,
the pattern of a shell, a puzzle of late leaves.

I noticed the scalloped curve of it, a vitality
in its arcing that held for days, though in time
the snake flattened out, dried up, turned gray
and then the colors of the dirty sand death bed.

Yesterday I saw it was in pieces. Today the flies
were feasting there and the snake was more
a shadow of its former shape, but still
I saw it whole even while the blue-black flies
carried off small shreds of a dim absent spiral.

This evening's rain will surely wash my memory
of the turn of it, and tomorrow there will likely be
no trace, except I know how the road curves there,
how a space can cradle breath, a present
and an evanescent thing, how the wind returns
the sameness and a difference.

Car Advertising Alligator Farm

Clamped to the front of a 1936 Chrysler sedan:
an embalmed alligator, upright, waxy belly
exposed, back legs spread and shackled, tail sawed
off, stump curled into a metal brace. Its glass
eyes, amber, gold, fixed in the sockets so they
don't roll but stare past the car's bulging
lights at the maracas strapped to each claw. Its jaws
are hinged open, as though it's singing. Long
after this car became obsolete, my brother and I
carried home a pail of baby alligators from a roadside
stand. We tipped it, chased gators across sandspurs
in tawny Bermuda grass of that distant
summer yard. I trapped one against the chain-link
fence, tiny jaws snapping, chased it over and over
until Daddy drove to the swamp and made us set
them loose among cypress stumps and purple
hyacinths because just that day he heard on
the radio about a boy falling into an alligator
pit at the Paradise Souvenir Shop and Alligator
Farm. A witness said the boy floated down,
hands unfolding slowly, revealing something tender
and secret in his palms. The boy eager, expectant,
in his white linen sailor suit, as if the meeting
with the gator was inevitable, something he had
always planned to do on a cloudless summer
morning. As if he knew one day he would be in
a poem about alligators. This strangeness he sacrificed
himself to, this appalling beauty.

jackrabbit: sixteen

An hour or so before first light,
fast distancing from the dark
of the old bunkhouse

acrid and delicious
my throat, my lips
my slightly glistening teeth:
semen reek of violation

prairie air sucks my breath
into vaster space

an affront to the Methodist night.

Across the ruts the headlights blast
gray-white intensity:
a jackrabbit running, racing the black,
light-producing car –
taunting, playful.

To the right, to the left,
back right, forward
a few leaps,
a delayed dash left.

One sound hanging: deep, laden thud.

East light as soft as rabbit fur
makes visible the gray fence posts,
the stretched barb lines marking
pitch barrow from burgeon field:
its far edge in yellow-red spasm.

Memories of Corn

The scent as you enter
the field, the itch of pollen
on sweaty flesh, how
the green leaves slash,
walking between rows
in early August, pale
silk darkening from
swelling husks, and
the heat, the heat in that
shade the tall stalks
make: tropical, deepest
jungle closing in on
a boy walking in corn
before returning to air.

Farming Below Sea Level

This was once the Sea of Cortez.
Now the air is lousy with lost seabirds
and prayer. Viscous. Thickened
with the motions of the slowest angels,
as if they were swimming in sweet, heavy beer.

It's not thin air, into which things disappear,
it's pressurized. You can feel
that the ocean has changed its mind, turned around
and is now bearing down on this desert.
The ocean says you will be baptized.

To be baptized is to fall
like a meteor through a blue atmosphere
or to descend into a body
stair by stair, or into a field:
a round bowl full of green air.
Some wild sunflowers. A white owl
in the towering cottonwood. Night unwinds
like a bolt of black satin.

How can a farmer, kneeling in his field,
find himself both worn-out and unborn?
It's not a new life, or an afterlife,
but the one unlistened to he's farming now,
hands cupped: a chalice
holding air, as if listening
is what air is for.

No moon. Pitch black. If you like,
read: these are fearsome times.
We are falling through the air
and we are feathered on the inside.

The special one

I remember the boy on the rooftop
loosing his pigeons into the charred night sky
smeared with neon, rancid with soot,
The oven door of a summer open on his face
and the birds a pastel banner flapping,
unfurling and tightening as they wheeled
as one body over East Harlem, 1970.

I remember a girl on a rooftop in Thessaloniki
feeding her doves, then letting them fly
up over the half crumbled ramparts.
Steep crooked houses crouched against them,
the night, a deep dirty pocket of heat.
I heard her calling their names, half singing,
Lily, Darling, Handsome One, Star Chaser.

Sometimes on the upper west side of New York
in a pecking, milling crowd of dirty gray pigeons,
there struts a bird of spangled feathers,
a white dove, a bird crested or crowned,
a bird who took seriously the promise
of freedom tossed from its rooftop cage.

That boy who dreamed himself a drug
lord, big car, new house for his momma,
fine clothes and no bills that could not be paid
bled his life in an alley among dog shit,
fast food wrappers and empties.

That girl got pregnant by a boyfriend
who ran away to sea on a freighter,
beaten by her brother, thrown out
by her father, died slowly of AIDS
in a narrow room under a roof where
a kid kept pigeons who cooed for her.
They were the last thing she heard
as her ears filled with blood, doves
who rippled as one flock and returned,
but not the special one who got away.

Holding Ava

My daughter has no jaw, my brother says
after the ultrasound. His voice through the phone
thickened by distance. They don't know
if they can operate. It's wait and see
and he is holding his breath.

Outside wind breathes over a burnished patch
of wood fern. My frail astilbe yield and almost break
beneath even the weight of air. Maybe doctors
are wrong, I tell him. Pictures lie.
He says her name in a whisper. *Ava*.

When she is born, he'll walk over
to where nurses are tending her, wanting
whatever he can have of his daughter's life.
After, he'll tell me about her fine hair and slender
legs, and the delicate mesh

where her jaw should have been. How
just after her heart stopped, he took a photograph:
mother and child on a white cotton blanket.
His wife left the room and he waited,
puzzling on the ways

his baby looked like him, the ways
she did not.
The tiniest bundle, he'll say,
and how he held her
even after the nurse came.

Burlap Sack

A person is full of sorrow
the way a burlap sack is full of stones or sand.
We say, "Hand me the sack,"
but we get the weight.
Heavier if left out in the rain.
To think that the stones or sand are the self is an error.
To think that grief is the self is an error.
Self carries grief as a pack mule carries the side bags,
being careful between the trees to leave extra room.
The mule is not the load of ropes and nails and axes.
The self is not the miner nor builder nor driver.
What would it be to take the bride
and leave behind the heavy dowry?
To let the thin-ribbed mule browse in tall grasses,
its long ears waggling like the tails of two happy dogs?

Obscure Longings

It is not detachment she wants. It is
what she would consider a sane mind; the
sharing of a fag in front of a stone
fireplace without her thoughts drifitng to the empty
beaches, the peopleless out-of-season houses,
the madmen who wander through the scrub
pine in the rain (in her childhood fantasies) looking
for contentedness in order to destroy it with a whack.
It is not an inability to face facts of
some despair she longs for or to replace
understanding with naivete; it is that she wants
to close out for a while the banging shutters, the
worlds beyond the burning driftwood, a piercing light
through the fog at the edge of the dune. She
wants to reflect only those visible
things and not confuse issues with the pain they bring.

Sweet Reveille On 54th

A ricochet of horn
skims its water-strider of sound across
dawn light on curtained glass
walls of my canyon. Leaning from
my morning window I
can't see him, but the glancing notes
dance on all surfaces
to make a ballroom of our building
cliffs with glissading phrases.
Now I can see the silver gleam
of horn. A Gabriel
upon a low roof, at an imagined
corner of the round
world, he blows into the ripening
blush of a New York summer
morning, trumpets *Body and Soul*.

Memorize This

We wore gloves
as if visiting a hospital room
but it was only a storefront
full of needles and tin cans.
Where was his harmonica?
You looked at me
 as if I knew.
Memorize this.
Memorize this.
Everyone but us
will forget.
You'd asked me there
to sort through his clothes and papers
before the newspapers found something bad,
before the landlords and health officials cleaned it all out.
Curses and pornography dripped down the walls.
Where were his cartoons?
You wanted me to find them.
Memorize this.
Memorize this.
Everyone but us
will forget.

The garbage and filth lined the floors,
fast food containers were piled in crooked towers.
Rusty broken parts of toys and
Instruments,
notebooks filled with lettering from
languages that never were.
You said – all of it was sacred – all of
it meant something.
Memorize this.
Memorize this.
Everyone but us
will forget.
You were pale–there was so much going on,
so many years of madness and mystery.
I hadn't even been born and you loved him so much.
"Why did I ask you here," you said to me.
"I shouldn't have asked you here." You lowered your eyes.
I tried to sweep. To clean and gather.
To organize the pain.
Memorize this.
Memorize this.
Everyone but us
will forget.
He had been your brother,
and I am your brother now.
Memorize this.
Memorize this.
      Everyone but us will forget.
      Everyone but us will forget.

Swing Dancing in The Blind Pig

Ann Arbor, Michigan

Resurrected from a past when a ghost
drank and collapsed against a pillar,
or slipped into what he must have believed
was a pew in a train station open all night,
this music couples dance to
could have, in another state, another time,
roped and broken every horse buried under
the collapsed barn that burned down. The man

who built it burned too, ashes a boy
sticks his fingers in before he touches
the terrifying mystery of
the girl's naked body. It's not just
the music, which could be a soundtrack
for a movie the couples, dressed for
a decade they weren't alive for,
must believe is being filmed tonight. It is

that there's a ghost who didn't pay to get in,
all his cash soot on the raw back
of some girl who wants music to play
and drown out the harsh hay and dust
drifting down her body. Some things should be
abandoned. Ghost horses whinny in the dust,
and the girl believes she hears them. They make
her feel more than this filthy boy

pushing into her body will bother to.
The dead do have advantages over
the living, it turns out. Maybe that is
what nostalgia is: not a longing for
the past, but for what the dead have
that we don't. Swing,
they call the music, and, when they dance,
it's a supplication for what's been lost.

*

Ask the ghost sitting on the burned stumps
of hands in a pew in the boarded-up train station
if dancing with a woman
charred those hands, if it was worth it. Horses
snuffle his poor legs, but his ghost hands,
if they do hold sugar, are under
some girl a boy's trying to touch the way
he's heard it's done. He's drawn some figures

on her flesh in ash – a man, a woman,
and some horses that burn inside her now,
where dry grasses could catch and turn everything
into ash with nothing to say about
resurrection. Nothing comes back
but what's lost. Swing, lovers, to music
that doesn't leave any ash and comforts
old horses who nuzzle a ghost for love.

Straw Houses

Never mind the smoke
wafting
from its
chimney –

If
poems are
like houses, built
from the roof down —- we have
just crashed
through to
the attic,
where, (whichever ones we've not broken,   yet) our toys
lay stored.   A fast flight
down
the
bannister
offers a tour through the runes of our imaginations: dead
or alive, familiar as that one   fine   flannel shirt   in the
parlor room closet...*(mmhhh)*
or, improbable
as the thought of finishing *anything*,   once begun.

Out the door: we arrive in the
garden, bang-bursting with the fragrance of roses & honeysuckle/marigold &
gardenia. Smell them.....
can't you?   *No?*   (nor, can i)   Their aromas, overpowered
         by that
                         what?,
                                emanating

                                from the cellar: dark, dank,
                                caliginous. That sickening-
                                ly sweet certainty that *this*
                                poem — is the last: every
                                comma, a trigger; each long
                                languorous loop ——

                                         a

                                    noose

Rat

Those things you never forget: waking up
In a friend's west side apartment, somewhere
way uptown on top of the alarm clock,
its red digits, five-o-something, a pair

of dim, red lights – eyes of a rat glowing
over me, frozen, just awake on the bed;
the feel of my brother's cold skin, laid out
on the city medical examiner's

table. Positive identification,
old scars that my brother had shown me
on his wrists, something he had to do to get
a bed in Bellevue, "that, or freeze to death

on the Bowery." Endless morning of the rat,
cold-as-hell first light outside, the taxi
flying me south, toward trains, toward Jersey,
my abandoned tan beret beneath the bed.

А.К.

Тебе еще страшно, моя непутевая бэби?
Немного Господнего хлеба и ложка вина.
Представь, расположимся мы в Парадизе, на небе,
И будет оттуда вся наша наличность видна.
Все то, что растратили мы, раздарили, раскрали,
Внизу заблестит, словно птицы железной помёт.
А гордые ангелы, эти бесполые крали,
Опять замешают на желчи лазоревый мед,
Который вольют в твое нежное алое горло.
Ты станешь нема и послушна, слаба и мала.
Забудешь, кого ты желала и чем ты была,
Измученный город, в котором со мною жила.
Тебе еще страшно? А мне уже странно и горько.

to A.K.

Are you still frightened, my clueless devochka?
Take a morsel of the Lord's bread (and a spoonful of wine, no?)
Imagine how we will reside in Paradise, in the skies,
and how we (finally) will see every thing –
our currency, all we have lost or stolen on Earth
will glitter below: like the minute droppings of an iron bird.
And the proud angels, those tall sexless bitches,
will again blend into their ruthlessness the sweetest honey,
which they will pour down your throat, your exquisite throat.
And you are now mute and cautious, now small and tranquil,
now you will forget what you desired, now,
who you were, now, this lamentable city
where we have lived together.
Are you still frightened, girl? Already I am a bitter stranger.

translation by Ilya Kaminsky, Rachel Galvin, and Kathyrn Farris

White Plumtree: Late Spring

The only thing worth repeating this Spring

Is the white plumtree struck among the ghostly yarrow

And ginseng patch just shy of Li-shan, Blue Mountain,

And how the fluttery redfreckled blossoms grew freshbreath in the night,

Knew every new Spring night, and broke early one May morning

Before dawn, beneath the sullen China moon,

Deadhard, saltsweet, jadecold.

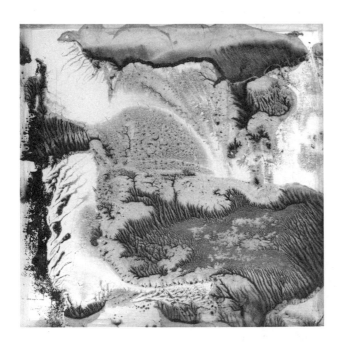

Am I Allowed To Ask My Book Whether It's True I Wrote It?

It must have been someone else,
someone out-of-control.
This volume is elusive as carp
in a pond. I dip into it,
but past the shiny surface,
purple restlessness and broken borders,
always the dark surprise.
Secrets held close, like those
folded in pleats of a Japanese fan –

waterfall, bridge, forbidden tryst.
Or in petroglyphs. Does that one mean
sun or drought? Does the one below
mean cloud or storm?
And the lovers notched in stone,
are they moving together or apart?
Book, fan, petroglyph: each one
an old mystery to decode.

Carp skim with such idle beauty.
For an instant I see through
their fish eyes, but later
what I knew is only an echo of an echo.
Who was I at twenty? At forty?
Who wrote these words?
If we were reintroduced,
would I be face-to-face with
a friend or an unmeasured stranger?

Title is from **The Book of Questions**, by Pablo Neruda, poem XXI.

Hwtsiil Tidangiyaanen

Tadlzuun tl'ogh k'eltsiini tl'ogh dghelaay cene'
tehwdeldiyna da'snidaetl natu'.

Pedni tehwedeldiyna nilk'aedze' ghot'
tse sdaghaay ogltsii;

tse Saghani Ggaay 'cen'iis nek'e 'et nekeghaltaexi',
tse kayaxygge ogltssi tabaaghe k'eze.

Pghatsiitsen baes hwlsiil, c'etiyi ya'atse
k'e dghelaay cene' k'eze tehwdeldiyna

yenka dldaek ts'ilghu,
yen dldaek.

Pghak'ae luk'ae i'nilaex, c'etiyi nic'ayilaan glts'aek'e
'uyuunistl'en hwna yanlae baa yikaa.

Weir Fisher

Flowing out of green foothills
the shallow stream enters the sea.

It began its winding course
long before these banks were cut;

before Raven stole the stars and moon,
when no village stood along these shores.

Below the stone weir, an old man waits
like the hills along the creek

for what the stream will soon bring
or what it will take away.

Once They arrive, he will lift his thin spear
while gray clouds slow the speed of light.

Light On Inishfarnard

The stripe that runs through these green stones matches
the light that falls on Inishfarnard today. The island slips
in and out of view through no movement of its own,
but from a massive rain that drives down
and sideways.

                The water between is flecked by wind that blows
even birds off their mindful course. Strange to see a crow facing
one direction and pushed another despite its feathered hinging,
though perhaps it reckons this while it tacks from here

to elsewhere. The celadon stones thrown ashore
weigh less than their slate or brown companions.
I do not know what laddered mineral constitution
makes them so, or more common than the rest.
They mimic the sun's crystal slash and twist

when its luster sieves in shafts through any thick weather
to skim the stubble of that smaller island, deserted for years,
anchored near this broader stretch of green.

                                        Was it excess solitude?
Or perhaps the fierce desire for place marking the sea-bound band
was not enough to hold, so they sailed away for good.

Their rock houses separate, working themselves to ground.
Choppy currents keep me from them: this season
favors a gale. Always a chance to retrace, if someone
can steer a fragile assemblage of bent wood; if I can find
my way across the short stretch of water to that abandoned
island gliding in and out of sight.

                                        When I walk the strand
again today, the beveled horizon starts to drift. Shifting
and drenched, it lifts anchor and dissolves into braids of mist.

The Stones of Memory

The stones of memory are different geologies.
Some are river rocks torn loose
by the current of a full flood,
tumbled over and around until all that's left
is a generic tale of time passing
and rhythms reduced.
                         Some are slippers of chert
on which you get no footing,
and which skip out of the mind
like a ferret, sneaky and apt to disappear
just when you think to grasp it:
                         the chert, the weasel, the memory
bounding, leaping down hillsides
ever out of reach – leaving
hints, occasional glimpses and then gone.
                         Or pegmatite, sharp edged –
no end of pounding can soften its granite jags.
Unlikely to move or reveal its underside,
these rocks are full of what you will tell
grandchildren,
                         small beings that know
before you do, that you are old as hills,
and give the same weight and distance
as the mountains that loom behind their house –

What can I tell
of how it was, or will be for them.
They won't believe. I didn't.

Yet, cranking ice cream
to get that sweet taste of summer on the tongue;
a cart pulled by a horse, the only way to get
from the aunts' – to the cabins on the lake.
What will they tell?

One asks if his father
could do a 360 on his skateboard, a 720, a 900,
something *his* heroes do every day. What kind of geode
holds the holds the memories of his father.

I am interested in their geology,
their mother lode two generations removed,
topo-map to their drives and fears.

What kind of ghosts will they see?
Who whispers in their ears,
and what kind of pebbles will tumble

in the speech of their curiosities?

Silencio

Ya no la escucharé

Porque todo lo que olvido
cae al mar.

Al corazón solitario del mar
donde mora, inquieto
el silencio.

Silence

I will stop listening to it.

Because everything I forget
falls into the sea.

Into the sea's solitary heart
wherein dwells a restless
silence.

Werewolf Lemonade

It's the humidity. The heat.
The way night drips over the end of day
slow and mysterious; how darkness pools
in coagulations across a wounded lawn,
under tired trees that thirst deeply
into graves of those who have died from it.

I take a long, iced drink of moonlight with lemon.
The glass sweats. Glistens. Blood rises.
It's a certain kind of moon, a certain sort of weed
blooming small white moths that float around
the old gypsy woman and Lon Chaney, Jr.

A meeting is called to decide the fate of mankind.
Lemonade is served with bitter cookies.
Reflections of canines glint off the polished table.
Everyone has a lie to tell or a once-a-upon-a-time.
Sweat slips into the wounds and burns like crazy.
The slightest breeze of tongues, a long, continuous howl.

Cirque du Liz and Dick

Puerto Vallarta

Facing each other rather desperately –
his eye is like a star –
we stare and say, "Well, we have come this far."

She doesn't like the lizards, strewn
like dry white bones
all over everything.

Nor the way stiletto heels sink
in the soft Moroccan tile that is
ubiquitous.

He drinks, and looks so bloody handsome.
Who dya think he'll make love to, Mrs. Burton –
Sue Lyons or Ava Gardner?

She feels discarded, fooling with her pearls
in the reptile torpor of the Mexican
Riviera. Key grips always

booming away somewhere beyond the patio.
He wants to be with her in London,
eating lemon pies. He longs for

the old delightful tracking down of
gloves to match a blouse or
just her drag queen whimsy.

Here it's all *La vida no vale nada.*
Life is worth nothing.
Part of her is sorry she became

a public utility.
Part of him wants to do Hamlet again.
But he feels closer to Claudius,

marrying so quickly on top of the death
of the other marriage. A woman
is like glass, they say here:

always in danger.
Together,
they've renamed the town *Seething* –

They still have *that feeling of antenna* –
a quivering contact with each other.
Above her head she poses

another spray of artificial roses,
making him think of a novelty rodeo act
he saw a very long time ago in Wales.

Nightgown

I remember the first time.
Her nightgown on the bathroom door,
lace blue, headstrong,
arms still folded at the elbows
to prove she'd been there:
a body, at night, with my father.
I remember first seeing
the woman that lived inside:
heavy against the door frame,
against my father, arms
rough and muscled –
like her lips the first time
I was told in my ear
to kiss them.

Grand Canyon

A strange man has taken our mother's arm
　　　　and led her into the lodge where there is music
　　　　　　　　and soft orange lights in every window.
We're in the back of the station wagon
　　　　in our sleeping bags, making up
　　　　　　　　a game. Pines wave against a jet sky
while the night cools down where Sputnik
　　　　makes another orbit. From what planet,
　　　　　　　　you ask, will be the first invasion? But I still
have not yet begun to believe in life beyond
　　　　the Southwest, where we have become trapped
　　　　　　　　inside camper trailers, silver and sleek, sliding
through the desert air, destined toward a thin
　　　　mountain atmosphere and an awe-filled hole
　　　　　　　　in the crust of everything knowable. This morning
we rested our fingers on the ridges of fossils
　　　　and imagined the sea rising to fill the canyon.
　　　　　　　　Where would we run? If now we saw a wall of ocean,
who would go inside to fetch Mother? Would she try to save
　　　　her children while her man-friend ran after her
　　　　　　　　or would she stay inside, accepting the next dance?
Our father taught us all the sugar drop songs of the first
　　　　part of the century. We sing them as the night orbits
　　　　　　　　around us and we look up through the car windows
where stars are multiplying. A million years ago
　　　　when waters subsided, a little stream continued
　　　　　　　　a mile below where it still spills muddily in the darkness,
far from ear's reach, though we can hear it clear as the wind.

Finally No Evidence

A latex glove in the dirty snow. Plastic quart-size coke classic
half buried. Shreds caught in baretwigged limbs. She falls
on ice. A young man

                         no thanks. I'm fine. Does he think
her forced smile
                         how old? When she looks in the mirror her lipstick

mouth blurs. On chapped lips color wantonly
traveling the fine creases. Roughly she
rubs her mouth. Roughly
again. Finally no evidence
of silly desire.

What kind of life is this
this ripe this
smooth this unhurrying
                         ascent and descent

quiet soles slapping shining wood floors
first to go up then
                         to come down. The faint
dog bark. The faint hammer's
lift and strike.

Lunch:
Soft rolls with thin ham

butter without salt. The butter cookie called Little Scholar
with gleaming chocolate

waxlike impression of an antique boy
caught running.

Pillows of snow creeping toward
light. Houses show themselves only by windows,

light they conceal.

High and deep
in the dark sky a sliver

radiant moon. Behind one window
a woman studying her hands.

The wind's harder breathing
stuttering the window frame.   A limited
war. Its limited
deaths.
          Soon

a few months the leaves again
budding. All that
murderous flourishing.

Collect for the First Sunday
of the Third Year in a Foreign Land

Grant, O God, that when I return
I will remember the language of my bunionned grandmother
Rolling towards me to run her calloused thumbs up and down my arms.
Grant that the soles of my feet
Will still be thick enough to smother the flames of the October sun,
Seeping through silk silt red iron
Bleeding earth.
Grant that my eyes
Will water each time I look at a musasa's leaves –
Virgins clinging to the black bark –
And that they might stay dry
In the smoke of a kitchen kwamusha.
Grant that I will still remember
The names of my cattle,
And how to explain that at age six
It was beyond belief that
Sekuru, the source of all running, gurgling, dripping joy,
Would give to my brother
What he would not give to me.
Grant, O Mwari of the heavens,
That I will be able to taste the soup
Of my Ancestors
As I chew on the slaughtered liver
And hear their voices proud
In the empty pod
Cowbell sounds of the mbira.

Grant that I will not notice
The smell of a hundred comrades
In a co-operatively-owned bus
But breathe the mists of head-held baskets
Stuffed with mangos, fowl, sweet potatoes, maize,
Yes, roasting maize, before I breathe the exhaust fumes.
Grant that I will not get lost
But like a sleepwalker in the native land, run blind but sure
Through the labyrinth of stripped and graying township paths,
To the concrete prism home
Of my Tete and my crowded cousins.
Grant, O God of Un-nameable Power,
That I will answer when they call me:
Tsitsi, maduve,
Musikana, wamazvimbakupa,
Muzukuru, Mainini, Muninina,
Daughter of the soil,
Daughter of the soil,
Daughter of the soil,
Stay with us a while.

Glossary (Shona terms from Zimbabwe):
Musasa: tree which sprouts red leaves in the Southern Hemisphere's spring. Mwari: supreme God.
Kwamusha: at the ancestral homestead. Sekuru: Grandfather.
Mbira: traditional Shona musical instrument (thumb piano). Tete: aunt (sister of father).
Maduve: zebra (praise name for women).
Musikana wamazvimbakupa (daughter of one who loves to give, praise name).
Muzukuru: niece/nephew, grandchild. Mainini: little mother. Muninina: little sister.

Coming Home

Who will hear us, who will come?
Who will take us home?
–Vahan Derian

1. boy/hunger (Somalia)

stare boy into the sky/black/dark/crows
                          lift from the branches
into his eyes days of iridescent wings hush wingsing
into existence. hushhush (Hush.   ) hushtheboy The boy
with flies in his eyes for stars. Beneath his mother's
shrunken hardberries, hardberries i(s) asleep forever.
Boy, girl, it's dark, come home.

2. the house

too silent and slow implosion/
                     the house
plowed under/
            absence startling as presence

someone lingering near the threshold
her face as full of longing
as the space around a body.

3. the search

I search for a home
That existed in time
Before the dark sorrow.
Cool grass crept to its waist.
And the waist of a woman
(Is it she?)
Like small *o*
Tightens in the curve
Of Darkness.
Her breathlessness
Gathers me home.

4. after visiting the Holocaust Museum

Let a new morning's light open my closed eyes.
Death, is that you here? Good Morning.
Or should I say Good Dark?
–Vahan Tekevan

I search for a thing that existed in time,
before the dark sorrow, when I was a man
      and alive.

     I remember the house
         as though it were tomorrow
and I were living there again: a luminous arc in the curve
of space, its pure articulation. It isn't a name

   – for the house near Sighet had no name,
     unless it be "our house" –
              but

    a return to plenitude: the startle before desire.

It is not a desire
for the old objects
in a new place, a new body
(for there is no place for a body to lie down here:
the body existed
before,
only there
)
but a matter of tracing the curve
to the lintel
the threshold: how among the space
s and near the place I walked each day
there might come a woman

leaning from

a window:
mother
sister
daughter

lover –

                   gazing   at blossoms
              tight as prayers
         in the garden
                   below. It is she, I say,
         ruffles lace at the sill with the curve of her
breath, a turn of the waist; the gestures as sure of a small
ex

         -clamation
                              oh
                         as the day's cerulean surrender
to the dark
         where I stand
      on the threshold
   (it was a house of breathlessness)
                                        of the dark
                                             hole the
secret swift and silent
                   implosion
                   swallowed into itself

                         the earth
                         as though
                              it had never been:
                              (Nor I. I
didn't.   I don't
              exist.)

                   uprooted, memory clinging as the shadow
                                   of a
                              body, a dark golgotha/

5. Home

we have never craved nostalgia,
the backward glance toward nothing.
it is nothing like that: but this:
that a home, like a woman, a man,
has a right to exist,
bees lazing in plums' burst seams
' intoxicating breath,
cicadas lined up on the sill,
cool grass beneath the porch,

6.

and her face,
waiting
watching
calling:
girl
boy
it's dark
come home

Horseweed Grass and Plum Trees, April 1946:
A Hibakusha's Lament

It was a strange summer of black rain
falling on the living and the dead...

Morning light threads through small holes
where the shoji is torn and yellowing

I lie swaddled in threadbare silk quilts
Neighbors shun my demon-face eaten by keloids

The mirror is draped in black cloth
No child will ever yearn for my milk

I cannot bathe in the ofuro
tainted as burakumin, Koreans

Everyone wishes the past buried in stone   But I cannot...
How does one describe a city of nothingness?

Hands of leafless trees twisting upward from
ruins where nothing stands but skeletons of metal

A boat bearing the Emperor's portrait crosses
the Ota The wounded pray along its banks

They seem barely human – staggering, naked
flesh dangling like old rags

arms reaching out suppliant –
images of Jizo carved in stone along a road

In hospital, patients scrawled their names
on lobby walls in characters of blood

There are no words...

I was lost and borne by a battalion of ghosts...
Now, we survey every portion of our bodies

an undiscovered country The spots are
clusters of red and green stars lovely, fatal...

How did we live? We would stuff dumplings with
horseweed grass and acorn flour

I concentrated on the most ordinary things...
We never imagined it would happen here

Kenji, my brother, wasted to freezing bone in
a relocation camp in Manzanar

But the Americans would spare our lives...
It saddened me when I heard that

no plum trees and long grass would ever flower again But
mountains and rivers remain even

if the earth is fed with bones of the dead
Outside, there is a row of

thin smoke-blackened cherries
You can see the blossoms of early spring

They are flowing clouds of heaven

It can almost seem that way

In Parallel

In the dream,
her image from a photograph
taken across the world
hangs back to back
with mine – mobile pieces
over the baby's crib:
here is her hand, here are my eyes
here is our baby's foot.
Her language is an artifact on his tongue
as he bites down on the hard consonants
of his first English words-bus, bulldozer.
I can smell the banks of his river-Mekong –
a breeze on the surface disrupts
reflections of faces – the family he was born into.
The memory of his mother-tongue floats
up river and birds echo an old lament.
Does he see you
standing at the river's mouth,
long cotton skirt brushing your feet?
Does he see us back to back,
side to side, whispering to him
in unison?
Two mothers
turning and turning
and turning.

My Name is Alma

Alma – Medica House, Zenica, Bosnia Herzegovina, 1995.

The women carry my arms,
or I lean on the plaster.
I watch the window (wooden hands)
hold yellow birds. They fly through.

I sit on my bed. Listening. Listen.
I live in the skin. My bones are glass,
are mirrors, are my brothers,
are mouths that speak in my sleep.

The women feed me pills and eggs
to shine the glass but not the mirrors.
They want me to tell them
my name but not my brothers'.

And not the birds. Or the sky
that holds them. Not their names.
Never the ones my bones speak,
mouths open in sleep.

Island of Bones

Well, ok, the past stripped down, hardened
into something white. Heaps of it.

And gulls, arguing mildly over the bits of flesh,
swooping into a shirfting embroidery –

this way, no, this way –
as fabric changes its sheen
'when pulled. If there are spiders –

white ones, tiny,
making a slow music
over the freeway of ribs,

the strange erector sets curving together
like sad shells, as hollow (without love,

all triumph is hollow) –

think of the inside of a flute:
silver, cold, the fluted breath
that blows into it, a mouth a frozen kiss

but the air – specific, warm.
And it's over this island of bones that the vines
begin – begin

as we grab the past and blow
air into its hollow,
the birds be damned.

XXVIII

Mask. Ghost before, ghost behind, ghost beyond. The mask. The face of
The other, the witch, the saint, the madwo//man, the other, the thief, the whore,
The mother, the other. The mask of the son, the mask of the daughter, the good
Mask, the wooden mask, the porcelain mask, the flesh mask, flesh mask of
The self, the self's mask of the other self. The other. The mask. The culture's mask,
The lover's mask, the other's mask. Take the mask, break the mask. Shatter
The mask, unhinge the mask, flatter the mask, shatter the mask. Pieces of the self,
Mask of the mosaic. The mask welded to the self by order (social, familial, etc.) —
Impostors with no mask, the imposition of the mask passed on to you. A family
Mask, a family task. A mask to show the world you're the other, other than who
You really are. The other. Not. Yourself. Who? Who wears the Mask of the River,
The fluid self we honor like the passage of light across a page? Flatter the mask,
Shatter the mask. The mirror of the mask, the face shown on the raw inside
Of the mask. The harsh scent of the raw interior of the mask as it presses
Against your face. Flesh. The flesh of your face. The Face. Mask of flesh.
The carved wooden masks, papier mâché masks, those fragile porcelain masks —
The Venetian masks your ex-wife's lover & his own wife wore to your daughter's
Birthday party. The Venetian mask of Pulcinella hanging in your hallway,
The deep blood-devil sculpted & painted Venetian mask, its mouth pure cruelty,
That Byron wore one year to Carnivale — there still in the little rooms off
The Piazza di Spagna. The terror of the mask, the sweet delight. The mask of sex,

The mask of tenderness. The mask of power. The mask of rain. The sweet delight.
The mask of concern, the mask of circumstance. The mask of desire, the mask
Of fire. The mask of rain. The sweet delight. The Mask of the River, flowing.
The mask of the saint, the mask of the savior, the mask of the face, the face,
The other face which manifests itself in silence, the skull-hung
Mask of, washed-out mask of, carved-apple-skin mask of: fear, simple fear
At the disappearing of the face, off the face of this earth. The mask reflecting
Fear. The desire, again, for the ancient masks. The masks of Death, of Laughter.
The masks of Fertility, of Fortune. The masks of Gods, & the Gods' own masks
Handed down to the lucky or the damned. Or the once-lucky, damned. Masked.
My mask when I say, Listen to me. My mask, when I say, "mask." My mask
When I turn my face to the audience just before the lights go up in the black
Auditorium. My mask walking out into the crowd. My mask like a foot stepping
Out onto the flowing water.   The Yoruba masks. Chichita's masks, bought in Paris
When she first moved there, from Tzara & Breton & other Dada/Surrealists
Who'd "passed through their African phase." The Yoruba masks. How our masks
Reveal the excess within. How we exaggerate the ugly within. How we mask what
We make manifest in the mask. How we mask in ourselves what we make manifest
In others. How we manifest so little of the glory of the mask we seek. Yeats' masks.
The self yearning for its opposite, yanking on the mask of the other the way
A catcher does before he squats behind the plate, ready for the curve, fastball, any
Change-up or slider. Again: Yeats' masks. Yeats behind the plate, calling pitches.
The Igbo spirit masks. The Face. Frozen. The fear of the held features of the face,
The flesh gone rocky & stone. The self petrified. Gone to stone. The fear of

The petrified self. The desire for the Mask of the River. The fluid self. The self Held by the mask of water, the self let loose of its stone vision, stone visage. The mask of the transformation. The transfiguration. The mask of the face of God. There, we've said it. God's face shining out of the silence like a hymn. The mask of music, the mask of cloud. The mask of rain. The sweet delight. The mask of misery & the mask of sex. Janus/gender masks. Trans/mask. Living Masks of blood pulsing up the thighs. Down. The mask of forgiveness, the mask Of forgetting. Mask of flesh. Flesh. The face of your mother before her mother Was born, the mask of her weariness, the mask of her humor & ease. Mask of The transfiguration. Your face. The face: The Face. There, we've said it. The mask of silence, the mask of prayer. The mask of flesh. The sweet delight. The cat mask Vivienne loved. The cat mask abandoned by X as she left That world of midnights & whips. Masks of innocence, masks of pleasure. Mask Of what it means to be invisible in the world, mask of notice me, mask of hurt me, Mask of the obsession & its release. The mask of rain. The sweet new night. Mask Without features, mask with no mouth. Mask with closed eyes, mask of Homer Laughing. Mask of the Medusa. Keats' own death mask. Mask of the dying, Mask of the rising. Mask of the face of Jesus. Endless masks of the face of Jesus. Buddha masks. Vishnu masks. Mohammed masks. Masks of belief. Belief's Masked masks. Masks of the eyes closed, masks of the visionary. Blake's mask. Raphael's mask. The mask of music, the mask of prayer. The mask of praise & the mask of gratitude. The mask of the inside of the mask, revealed. Flesh. The mask of reckonings, the mask of desire. The mask of pure adulthood. Your mask. Your face: The Face. There, we've said it. The sweet delight.

from *The Face*

Light is Faster than the Knife

Little atom, Father on the wall,
scratch our names on scraps of light
that shoot out, into eyes.

The one way to destroy a name is to destroy
the one it's written on. When names are
scraped away a knife is pushed into our eyes.

But Father, light that touched our eyes
reflects, and pushes out into another's eyes
and so the name survives

and so a knife is pushed into those eyes.
But still, the light from those
pushes out into another's, eye to eye,

and knife to eye, but always light
is faster than the knife, and names
get strung from eye to pushed to eye to eye

until we're sewn together
in a cloth of names so permanent and light
it rises, covers all our heads, and is unseen

like everything that keeps us here alive: the air,
the possibility of love, our people
who were somewhere else

and someone else's people
their eyes inside my eyes
looking out at our forgetting.

Aphrodisiac

He'd know the winner as if personally in charge of him,
the pit crew of a boxer or, more likely, the fan who'd seen it all,
set beguilingly in the wide orphanage of trees.
Snake vs. the alligator was a common one we'd discuss
in the evening of a living room, Safari Cards in hand,
our feet stuck to the bottom of Nile, mud over our memory,
the green earth, suddenly covering me in the net of history.
It never mattered who won, the remembering the aphrodisiac,
the certain conduit of leash. With my grandfather,
the living almanac of beasts, I'd pair
the ultimate contest in safari heat: *snake vs. lion*,
one, the king of the forest, the other, master of sleep,
and slowly it would come over him, the poison from the fangs
the incision from the cut just deep enough to enter the stream
to the heart of the thing, which then, he said,
would harden in its drowsiness and, almost apathetically,
drift away in royal defeat, end up a carcass in the plains,
like genocide victims, for the vultures to eat.

Within the Pale

Within the pale of settlement three old men rode
Horses backwards into stables consumed with fire.
I am reading this into an empty night filled
Only with rotten stars. I would go singing with
My fellow Hasids if I knew their songs or they
Knew mine. I'd give my right foot to be devout, I
Told the parson who thought I was lying. I chose
Not to confuse him with my shreds of truth, which I
Pushed back into my pockets and rambled on. It
Was almost time to make *shabbos*. I would not reach
My shtetl in time. Paler than white ink I'd be
Found, poured over an unhallowed ground, already
Dissipating with the dew.

                        I arranged to have
Myself stand bootless in the middle of a chalk
Circle, each big toe touching the point of a five-
Pointed star. I waited for wind to start howling,
For the moon to be eclipsed, for my patience with
Life to wear thin as the air in a lecture hall
Where the state of the planet is being discussed.

God! Was there never anywhere I could belong?

sssssssssssssh.   sssssssssssssssssh.

if you sssssssssssssh i'll tell you when

we found the lynched boys

restrung them in the leaves

hidden cherubs   /   tourist canopies

we rehung them in the trees

nobody knows

they sing when it breeze

the neighborhood knows

sssssssssssssssh.

Waiting for the Birds to Talk

Silk nets, troubled wings,
slipknots, tricks they say no bird
can untie, the soft binds, a mother's arms,
the strips of a cotton pillowcase
that once cuffed your wrist. Thoughts
you can't shake, bound wings,
figures wrapped and cast into voicelessness,
feathers and the endless thoughts
of feathers, old pillows, feather beds,
feather fights, the geese your grandmother plucked,
the downy snow of the bodies –
No – your feathered body falling
to the floor of a jail cell in Selma,
no the memory of a feather pillow breaking
over the head of a younger brother –
No – a memory of a feather pillow cut open
in a search for a hidden book, the memory of a yellow finch
feather the summer your great grandmother
eyed a carriage, said three words and spit, and the horses
stopped by the cemetery and would not move
No – a jail cell in Selma where there are
no pillows, no birds, just what's left
of your breath, the low beginnings
of an undying warble, its sweet persistence.

1913

(After Ernst Kirchner's *Berlin Street Scene*)

something was about to be accomplished:
      a boot-heel poised above
the shovel's edge, smoke from a genie-bottle
      glimpsed, the renunciation
of an adage (this is history as summation,
      gavel-tapping proclamations) a kink
knocked loose from the ancestral chain:

Berlin: 1913: Kirchner's at his window again,
      looking playfully down the sight-line
of a brush, preparing to paint
      the error in: bolt in the cartwheel
loosening, a wind-tipped spittoon,
      the pickpocket drumming
his fingers on the railing: this is randomness

(what Kirchner calls the eenie-miney-moe
      of the mind) refigured, almost
perfectly, into moderness: the world made up in uni-
      form: the green helmeted boys turtle
through the grass, and later, the colonel,
      in love with novelty, confirms the dead
by tapping each body with a piñata stick:

**

for three days – brushes forgotten in a dish
        of solvent, deflated air balloons
upon his pallet – he'd been refusing
        to paint: all color, he'd decided,
was a form of restraint: wax-drippings
        on an envelope, innuendo meant
to flush the cheek, meant to suffocate a face,

or Kirchner himself, thirteen years ago, painting
        a severed wing in pinks and greens
and nailing it to his mother's door: this
        is the day of the invention of X-ray,
of news, from United States, of a doctor who,
        using the machine, lowered a clamp
into a chest, and though the body had learned

to cling to it, pulled a nail from the darkness
        of a young boy's lung: how romantic,
Kirchner thinks, to paint like that, to do away
        with the exterior and look straight down
into the pain: this woman, for instance, walking
        home, straight-lined, lips like a diary-lock,
a scarf trailing down her back like a horse's mane,

if she carries in her purse, a choral
        soaked rag for lifting to the nose,
a way to forget more precisely, to trim
        back the bramble of the mind, if she thinks
of her own history as asphyxiation,
        even if he could lift the fingerprint
of consciousness from her gravid face,

soak her onto the tip of his brush and hoist
        her from the street, could he make audible
even one note of her *shivered prayer*, the secret anthem
        playing in her brain: no: all he can do
is add his deception to the scene:
        a bricklayer trying to wall
the horizon in, history smothered beneath

the ticker-tape of collective imagery:
        airplane photos, chalk-board strategy,
the boy who, he remembers, would recover fully,
        if you overlook the chronic tinge of something
rusted in his breath: now Kirchner turns
        from the window, he turns
towards the palette with the spotlight

of his brush: he must touch the canvas
        only once, he thinks, he must remember
only one thing, to put an end to possibility:
        he'll swirl pink and green feathers
through the woman's hair: *lord*, she sings, *let paradise*
        be clean when I arrive,
let it smell of paint-thinner, of formaldehyde.

Crystal Gazing

The glass set out
on the table
is an egg and anchor vessel
with a fish-eye bottom,
a stem and a foot
that my sloth's hands
can grip
and an orifice
that receives
the impress
of weaselly lips.
Wine and water,
making second
wavering rims
swim in it.
I drink like a fish,
thirsty and afraid.
Yet some water
evaporates;
some wine spills.
When I set down my glass,
the sun's slant
makes quicksand
of the table's face
and my mole's eyes
can't tell if this light
turns my chalice
into an aquarium
filled with scenes
from the past
or if it is the present's
hourglass.

Again Reading "Barbara"

Rappelle-toi Barbara
Il pleuvait sans cesse sur Brest ce jour-là
         – Jacques Prévert

Beside a spray of sunflowers
she sits rereading "Barbara."

Her lips draw the poem in
      one ongoing kiss from the air
      each word a monument.

She loves those who love
      even without knowing them
           and she aches for Barbara's lover
                  perhaps lost in the war.

It had rained incessantly in Brest that day, the day of the other Barbara.

She reads and wonders
        where the lovers were
                when the rain was gone, when the clouds
                        remained but the city was gone.

She repeats the name, Barbara, because it is hers
        foreign as metallic rains
        intimate as mourning.

Sunflowers mark a father's desk
                the black and gold
                        too definite
                                reducing all men to none.

She has known many kinds of loss.
She is learning many kinds of war.

In this one, sunflowers
        shed their petals
                it spits rain outside
                        and she has never been to Brest.

Tattoos

Oseh shalom bimromav
hu yaseh shalom aleynu
v'al kol Yisrael
v'imru, v'imru amen *

I got this tattoo in Budapest.
That's Buda-Pest. The s
like the s in schtick,
schnoz, schnockered, Pest.

I got this tattoo when I knew
There'd be no way to find
a relative in Budapest.

They changed my name.
I don't know who.
Some clerk,
some faceless official
in some faceless act.
A pen mark erased
my family name, a guttural
phlegm throng palate stirring name
I was told you had to throw up
to pronounce correctly,
but it was my name,
someone's name before me,
someone's name
who left brothers and sisters
with pennies for passage
bundled belongings in wicker
and old scraps of cloth
for the good life,
for me

and it is from them
I've inherited
this need to travel
across the seas, again.

I got this tattoo
in a city that still claps
to a rusty communist beat
in a city who recognized the me
for me, before me, before –

y'aseh shalom, y'aseh shalom
shalom aleynu v'al kol Yisrael
y'aseh shalom, y'aseh shalom
shalom aleynu v'al kol Yisrael

The me before me
whose name I wanted
to pronounce, whose name
I wanted to find
cousins, great aunts, cross borders
because for the first time
I felt close.

I felt close to my mother's
flat nose and almond eyes.
I felt close to her olive skin
and wild, curly, coal black hair.

I got this tattoo
in Budapest.
Had it scraped across
my right shoulder
in black ink.

Had it scraped across
because numbers
took my cousins.
Numbers
closed their shops.
Numbers
took them to not
grow old.

I do not
have numbers.
I do not
have numbers.
I got this tattoo
to remind myself
I do not have numbers –

y'aseh shalom
yaaseh shalom
shalom aleynu
v'al kol Yisrael

I came here by train.
They left here
by train. I'll leave here
by train, but I'll
be going home.

*The Hebrew transliterations are an
excerpt from the Mourner's Kaddish,
asking for peace.

Rising Sun

faded to bare flickers of pale color
       in brittle 8 millimeter film stock
my mother strolls Ginza streets
       soon after the war restored
young and thin as a corn stalk
       soon after my birth
behind her bulbous sedans in military tan
       slide past as she pauses
and shields her eyes against
       the mid-century light
I was born in a ruined land rising
       from bomb craters and earthquakes
smell of honey buckets carried away mornings
       to rice fields balanced on shoulders
steam rising from *onsen* waters
       snow flakes drifting down
mornings the river below hotel veranda
       muddy from earthquakes in the night
all the mountains volcanic
       and Fuji's calm a facade
old 8 millimeter film stock thin
       as my mother's hair
hips and torso thicker now and the air
       Tokyo mornings smells
of exhaust Ginza streets I have walked on
       gone the ruins of war
and economic miracles
       but still my mother young
walks shielding her eyes against the sun

அமைதிப் பேச்சுக்கள் கலந்த நாள் அன்று நா

காலை காய்கறி விற்பவனின் இசை நாடகம்
வாழைக்காய், வெண்டைக்காய், அவரைக்காய், வெ
வாழைக்காாாாாாாாாாாாாய்!

கோவில் ஆனையின் ஒய்யார நடை
அதன் காலில் சூட்டின கிண்கிணி ஒலி
வானமீன் மழைபோல் மாற்றம்

காலை வானொலியில் தமிழ் இசை மாலை
பூக்களின் நூற்று எட்டு நாமங்கள்
நாட்டு வீரர்கள் நலம் வேன்றி பாடல்

ஒரு பழமொழி:
மேலபோல் கடினங்கள் வரும்
காலை பனிபோல் அவைகள் மறையும்.

What I Heard the Day the Peace Talks Stumbled

Morning opera from the vegetable vendors:
Vazhakkai, vendikkai, avarakkai, vellarikkai. . . .
Vazhakkaaaaaai!

The lumbering gait of a temple elephant
translated into a starry rain
by two-tone bells hung on its feet

On the radio, a pushpanjali,
the recitation of one hundred and eight names
of flowers as a prayer for soldiers in danger

Also this, an old proverb:
Trouble may come like a mountain,
then disappear like dew.

*Tamil for plantains, okra, beans, cucumbers

Katsura

1959

He turns back to us in the shade
of the maple, slowly intoning – each
word precisely balanced in the green
repose of early afternoon
  Water   rock   moss   trees:
four elements of Japanese garden.
Bill's film cameras purring, Mary
muttering something about the pace,
our collective plans for a grand lunch
in the Gion vanishing with each
measured footfall. Still, from inside
the tea house – inside the smells
of cedar and straw grass matting,
we see where we've been – pieces
of pond, garden, framed new with
each sweep of shoji screen.

2002

Returning is a way of realigning
memory – a second level of
transparency laid down over the first,
the emerging image richer now,
greens deeper. Water rock moss trees:
no guide this time, but the mind
of the design itself – each turn
of the path calculated to focus the gaze:
now the curve of the bamboo gate,
now the drift of leaf shadow
in the shallows of the pond,
and at the top of the path, not
the sum of Imperial Kyoto below,
not the grand view of the whole
we'd come for, but the one stunted
pine that blocks it. Look here, it says –
to look here is everything.

Subcutaneous

I

It is strange how light
quickly fills up your body

like a clear glass bulb filled to the brim,
close to the point of breaking.

Here, you said, is a corner of pain,
less of a feeling

more like an aching thought
that rubs the seamless side of the brain.

II

When your old wrinkled hand
clutches the knife, cuts open

the brown heart of ripe nectarines,
I, too, expect the morning to burst

and flood into this room that bears
the stubborn scent of formaldehyde.

III

We simply repeat the motions.
One hand holding the door

one hand seeking the knob
of fear, plunging, subcutaneous.

The nurse taps the syringe, feels the pulse,
unlocks the sharpness of needles.

Last Gift

My great aunt Joy went to the bathroom
in Japan,
and on a board, with the weight of seventy years,
she fell into sewage.

Perhaps in wading new waters,
she found yin and yang
despite years of missionary, Methodist training
and a 1918 Kokomo, Indiana birth.

* * *

After my grandmother could no longer
diet by eating only pie,
she forgot my grandfather's name,
called him Joy
and chewed the air as if trying to gnaw
her way to Heaven.

An answer to prayer, divine
beauty fell her way.
It sunk her cheeks, paled
her skin to paste
and made her an apparition
of starched sheets with a halo
of white, wild hair.

When she died, she called God for Joy,
who never came.

* * *

As a last gift,
I kissed my grandmother
and placed a note in her coffin,
between the pages of a small, black Bible:
I am terribly sorry to inform you,
Miss Joy Clevenger has been unavoidably
detained in Tokyo. She is with God's
creatures, great and small,
bacterial and otherwise.

First Interview with My Corean Father

That morning, I lost the part in my hair.

So you were never able to finger the whorl again,

the one from which that froth of your hair began?

Maybe, but don't write it that way.

What did it look like?

I didn't carry anything in my shoes –

didn't take any of them with me either.

Then how did you walk once you crossed the river?

Actually, it wasn't a river.   Oh right, the Yellow Sea.

Well, how did you get across?

When the tide was out, I ran toward a different sun,

escaped over dogs of mud.

O-VER...MU-DDY...DOGS, okay. What else was left behind?

I was left behind, so was your grandmother and great-aunt

for four years, or so we thought.

But you said you were *South* Corean–

> *Not left behind, separated. From your grandfather.*
>
> *Go-saeng, so many hardships.*

Before or after you lost your whorl?

> *I told you that was secondary.*

I know, but you and mother still sweep with a broom and water.

> *Sometimes, I bore holes in my teeth hoping they'd be*
>
> *replaced. Other times, I suck on the old ones like mints.*

Why didn't you buy me a drum?

> I could've made some noise –

> *You were born with too many leaves in your belly.*
>
> *They looked too much like fried feathers*
>
> *and we thought you'd burst from the crackling.*

Paper Trees

My father has learned the terrible secret
of reading the splitting bark of winter
birch. He'll sit for hours weaving the gummed strips
of its white veneer through his fingers
as if there was something there they had both
earned (like the dark claw marks he's always carried
inside). Then the wine-sap bleeds from its throat
filled with language – slashed and fragmentary,

seeping into his cold meditation
like scenes he's trying to reclaim and curl
back. And I sit hypnotized by the rhythm
of the paper trees that bend him, their translation
of the foothold he once had on the world,
peeling off the coarse shell, releasing his vision.

Elderly, She Paints Another Nude

The mirror has teeth: even my tongue feels
wrinkled and skin that once was banned
in Boston hangs dry and spotty as those rags
I use to clean my brushes   O muse of Park-
inson's whose shaky hells advance like Meals
on Wheels upon all fronts   steady my hand
for one more work before the mirror cracks
and all these clamoring images go dark

There's room in ancient heads for dreams of youth
of either sex   bright eyes and satin skin:
impossible to let these phantoms rest!
They weave behind weak eyes that can't in truth
read the directions on my aspirin
but see with mnemonic clarity your breast

Aubade with Memory Crystallized
into a Figure of a Dancer

That night was spent searching for a form of fire. . . the street
lights spilled off your face – the corner of the room

fully flooded with blue, a sticky flame. Earlier,
we had found a picture book you kept when you were young

and you wondered aloud, "Who was that voice?"
She had wanted to be a dancer – she had wanted to be the moon.

Such an awkward grace, to be the moon. Sky-bald,
abandoned. Zero and sleepless it aches and is cold.

It is far from fire, yet you crave it as though the rage
of sizzling insects, if loud enough, could spur the sun.

How do you fathom it then? Childhood singled out. Ageless
in your pirouettes about the sky, gravity-less and wounded.

And who would she kiss, I ask, and who would she ache
or grieve? And are you still so small and flickering or is it the window

who makes this mistake? Is it the body's *battement* and *ballon* that vaults you
into the past, beyond sleep? We could not find your toe-shoes

among the childhood things you hid, though we kept ourselves awake
until dawn, searching because you had wanted them

and they had possessed you. They were just shoes but to you
a snare in the moment is everything. Nothing would convince you

otherwise. Not the hour or the way the hour begged you to stop.
Though this moment makes you the moon,

you cannot be that dancer, crystallized into the bluest body
of that sphere's deepest crevasse. Though there were rivers

on the moon once, the arch of your foot buckles
under the weight of your memory. The angels of the past

cannot be awakened through the turnings of a simple picture book
or the physical gleanings of the body recalling a moment

when it was airborne. Despite every aperture of the evening
turned to morning, this figure of you that you've memorized –

grande battement – would it recognize itself, flying, perhaps, or earthbound?
Even in daylight would she laugh? Would she flare?

Angelophony

This architecture of anguished angels,
A colonnade of white marble, arches
Of rain worn wings, pitted, pocked – stones
Act as guardians in the cemetery of Jewish angels,
Where angels mourn, weep before strangers, five
Stand bowed – See this stone
Staring down from above, who taught him pity? A stone
That wears the face of a boy? Read the broken grammar
Of the eyes: What syntax
Failed to spell his grief? Stones
Weep upon the wet, black leaves. My grandfather
Was not buried in this earth – my grandfather's

Hands of offering bread, now ashes. My grandmother
Reads the *New York Times*, Seraphim
Fold their wings around her chair. My grandmother
Hears her hands spell *go on*. My grandmother
Believes in the faith of hands, fingers arched
To make a steeple, the only church she'd claim, the grand
Sons who laugh upon her lap, the grandiloquent
Gestures of childhood: its constancy of light – *five
The age I always am in here*, she touches her chest – five
Hundred years of heart. My grandmother
Respects a garden. She speaks the grammar
Of good dirt and common sense, the grammar

Of my grandfather being gone, the grammar
Of *a life well lived is a long conversation*. Grandmother
Is a dactyl of *coming homes*. Grammar
Is the architecture of obedience. But what is the grammar
We are growing towards? Do the angels,
Those Beings of Light, *know* our sentence? As we conjugate
    the syntax
Of our souls? They fly inside the grammar
Of our grieving. They reside among the archipelagoes

Of the poor, the hungry, the alone. And the Arch
Angels, administrators for our suffering? That grammar
My grandfather worked his life to lessen – five
Is the numerology of the human face. My five

Year old wipes his eyes. Five
Times he asks *what is it to die?* There is a grammar
To the mice we bury in the backyard, the five
Crosses for five small lives – five
Times my son makes the same prayer, this grand
Gesture: *in the sky may they have friends.* Five
Rhymes with live. There are five
Stations to the cross, the last angel
With my grandfather lifts his eyes–who is this angel
Who weeps? My son holds up five
Fingers to show his age – Archimedes
Solves his equations. My grandfather denied
    the architecture

Of angels who spoke his mother's Hebrew name. The Arc
His mother walked towards when he was only five –
How many angels dance on the head of a pin? At the *Arc*
De Triumph my grandparents bent to kiss. Archibald
Macleish wrote *a poem should simply Be*. This is the
     grammar
Of a spider's web.   An architecture
Of strands, thin as light.   An *architecture*
Like a language. It was after the war, my grandfather
Studied Chinese, recited Mao, my grandfather
Studied the syntax of helping others live, the arch
Of human lives, the Angel
Of History bent her head to listen – what angel

Utters my grandfather's vowels – angel
Sifting light from ash and bone. This architecture
Of remembrance, a house of opening doors: I am five,
I hear the front door unlocking, hear the grammar
Of my grandfather's footsteps down the long hall.
My grandmother says, *He is always coming home.*

The Button

The button pops
ticks on the floor
rolls into silence.
The cloth falls away from the breast.
In the sudden cold the flesh stills
as if for flight.
The nipple is a star.

The old man my father
who has forgotten every thing
but not my mother
thrusts his hand inside her blouse.

In the Sixth Year of My Father's Illness

I wonder if he remembers the jay
that flew into the living room window

that first day he introduced himself
to the neighbor he'd known forty years.

It lay upon the crushed
pine bark we spread the previous May

around the roses where the roots were smooth
and thornless, that jay so blue and *too beautiful*

to move, he said. And it stayed beautiful
even as the ants paraded in and out of its head,

removing little bits to their underground country.
Afterwards its body lay still

and still beautiful, as if death had not yet
occurred to it, its feathers

blue as the sky it once knew so well,
that sky it mistook

for the real thing. Some truths
we cannot learn. Some we forget,

as my father did, who yesterday
introduced himself to me.

Work

That woman's mother has forgotten
everything: where
was she born, she does not know   whom
did she marry   what   ghost-blue love gaze
pummeled her fat hips,   who? what is your dear tall
skinny daughter's name? she has no
daughter damn
stars, and pigs, and
men, all men, am I a man? she does not speak
she does not know but she sings. all her songs.
all her recalled low notes,
dun sparrows, come home.
all her Hamburg *lieder*, all her mama's lullabies
in hoarse dark winter alto, all day, she sings a loop of
perfect pitch in German, is this *Deutschland?* what the
century and why she has her hands, her teeth, breasts,
why she has these, she forgets.

The soul wants attention and I don't know how to give it, what would be enough
applause, or eyes? Is naked good? My mirror has given up. I remember being
born. Everybody wanted a world that would remember. What is a woman permitted
to forget?

it's a game. what if epidemic. we are so much better prepared. but first you have to
agree to do the soul's work. an ex priest tells me that. do your soul's work. what am
I, then, allowed to forget?

The ex priest wears no robe.
The ex priest's mother
dies before the winter,
never forgetting, her son could have saved a country, but he chose woman.
The mother died in morning mass in church. She was singing. A blessing,
said the friar.

In his mother's velvet
salon, all night in the dark, her piano wakens him,
humming, in her empty room.

His mother
hated his wife. What priest leaves God,
to sing to a blonde?

If my soul has work to do, I dare not settle for a simulation. I've stood
in the unemployment line. My soul wants work.

House and Universe

The first walls are a great animal sleeping inside the sound of the heart. Sound of the rain. Breath.

The second walls are far like what is near in a fever. So far away there is no sense of wall, only odors and voices, and the very smallness of the self.

The third walls take you back to the first. To sleep. To dreams. And these are the walls you eventually fall from. This is when you learn what your lungs are for and how alone you are inside your pain.

The fourth walls are everywhere, and you can move among them, listening to the talk of a green bird in a cage. Or you lie on your back and turn them upside down and spend the evening alone and calling. Inside these walls are the spaces that might be yours. One day you make a little version of the world on a scale you can lean above. You stand in the hall with the green bird in the cage beside you, opening and closing the gate you've made in this world, and this is when you begin to know who you are.

The fifth walls are full of ghosts. When you sleep inside these walls it is hard to know which world you are walking in. These walls are old, and they are where your dreams will come from for a long time. Inside these walls you carry an invisible thing you don't yet know how to name, even when it greets you, resting its cold hand on your back as you climb the stairs. You don't speak of it, but each time you come back inside these walls, it moves close to you.

Inside the sixth walls you take your books, turning over each page where the invisible thing you carried home from the ghosts takes on voices and shapes and tells you stories about yourself. These walls are old and high, and here you discover how small a woman is supposed to be, and how big your ghosts are. You begin to write back to them and all the empty space you find you can fill with what you want to say,

and saying makes around you the seventh walls. Words that pull the white peaks of the sky together, a roof the rain now beats down on, that the creek rises beside. House of wind. House of water. Sound of the heart. The rain.

obituary, three drafts

I.

We lost gabrielle jesiolowski in the maze of cornrows
where she went running off   the sun had four corners that evening.
We found her hanging from the roof of a tree   her eyes colorless.

She would have liked the wind   all of the glass being thrown in
the alleyways   from the high rise apartment windows
                                         ~~after we lost her.~~

On October the 18th we will
let her ashes blow out the smoke stack of some ship
                    and we will all make love all night under the deck.
                    Lanterns will be hung on all masts.
                    ~~Waves will crash.~~

II.

She was killed, gabrielle jesiolowski, by sharks   lead color
Her hair, tangled in rough seaweed,
                ~~nineteen shells were found in her mouth~~

The great torso of wind took her away from us
like so many great winds   we do not know why...
Because of the deepness of the wounds
and the movies we rescued from her final days
                ~~8 mm abstractions of light and water~~
services will not be held at this time.

III.

Is that all there is? this jackknife of metal slicing by?
gabrielle jesiolowski   found dead yesterday in her swamp side shack
having *carved an entire opera into the pinewood door*   ~~swinging open.~~
We will carry her on that pinewood door   to the sea
empty her ~~body~~ into the wash of waves
singing opera in our most howling of voices   ~~always.~~

The Dead

We eat their ashes,
a little at a time
to make them last longer.

That's how the bodies of the living
become the graves of the dead.

Then, like Noh masters,
we project our shadows,
their shadows on the wall,

those shadows of shadows
we call memories.

And we make the dead
speak for us, say it's them,
filling the unbearable silence.

Jaguar

—after and with Rilke at the Jardin des Plantes, Paris November 2002

Pacing a trench
ankle deep, etching
deeper across a grill
of black shadow
crosshatching hapless
days

Course growls, mere feeble
groans, the depleted
song of exhausted jaws

His tongue a dried wafer
of whitening blood

A mute yellow tear
suspended as bronze, soldered
below his left eye,
the weight of surrender
written in pale fire–

The tug and gawk of
confused human stares
has singed a dying
light has crushed
a luminous truth

For Edgar Bowers

I said to you once, "Wasn't Henri lucky?
I'd like to go the easy way he went,
Suddenly, in the middle of the night."
And you replied, "Oh no, I want to *be* there."

And so you were. There, infinitely far

Memory is in our fingers

With you missing I forget what to do
with my hands. They give me away
shifting constantly and inspecting
one another
like a pair of lovers.

My hands wander my body
looking for your hands.
They groom, worry. They touch at my face,
compare it to your face,
find it wanting. Only in sleep

do they come back together. See how
they lie down near me; I wake
to their small
empty cradle.

The Vigil

I have seen them watching over us, settling
in the clouds above: my grandmother,
after her century on this earth,
in the arms of her husband who has waited
since the blackened skies of '36.
And generations of housecats
vexed by the white vapors of sparrows;
prize fighters pummeling the green
hillside in spring; blossoms
my children offered up
in their grass-stained palms,
blooming a second time overhead.

One loss billows out of another as
we remember how each spirit flies
like spit off the tongue.
Nimbus, stratus, cirro-velum,
the ancients knew them all.
They scattered salt to calm
the storms of the heavens and the flesh.
As a child, my grandmother sat
on the rain-splotched steps

and called up to her grandfather McCracken,
in the skies over Pittsburgh
to send down another gold coin
as proof of his presence.
And he let it fly, the pellets
of hail gleaming as they
slipped into her shoes and melted.

Whom should I call now,
the thrush or the pine bough
swallowing the mist? To the voice
which has left the lips of those
we loved and been orphaned in mid-air?
We slip from the clouds' grasp
as they drift south, leaving us behind.
Yet, even on days when the sky
weighs as much as a body being lowered,
there is a light between the stripped branches,
a radiance leaping off the bark,
and a stream of rain running to the end
of each twig, dropping into the emptiness
that seems to breathe again.

Legacies

FIELD HANDS

Maybe you're in from the field,
boots spattered with new-mown grass
– but that wouldn't have lasted
for centuries, and besides, the dead
have no odor other than the earth.
Yet I smell something raw, almost
animal, as I sense you reach for
my cup of black currant tea –
to warm yourself? But you have
no body. Even your bones are a ruin.
When I try to hear your voice,
syllables crumble like tilled earth,
the field stills, warm wind carries
threats of change and intrusion away.

PARLOR GAMES

In the photograph I have of you,
you wait to serve the noon meal –
a meat bone boiled with onion,
bitter turnip, maybe lemon grass.
You stand in the doorway, hand
shading your face, looking out
to the field. Late again. You go
to the parlor, the oval mirror, loosen
the pins from your hair, let it fall
fast as water. You spin, slowly,
a girl again. You hold your hands
over your breasts. So thin! You feel
your ribs, your hip blades. Is this
how desire rises again from nothing?

NIGHT STAND

At night, you sit in the rosewood
chair, reading my books, staring
at the photographs, wondering about
those who have come after you.
The other morning I noticed
the area rug, bunched up
like a desperate signal. Gently,
I smoothed it, half expecting it
to resist. I startled when the pattern –
arabesques in blue and brown –
taunted me with the increasingly
distinct outline of one shoe, another.

EAR TRUMPET

I do not fear you. I do not sit here
feeling your threat from the back,
thinking there are sins I must redeem,
hurts and betrayals not hidden at all
but full of discoverable intent.
When I saw the outline of your shoes,
I confess I balked a bit, shook
until I sat and thought, *One woman's
reality is another woman's ghost.*
As if you'd whispered the words
into my ear – they came that clear.

IRISH CURTAIN

Yesterday, the rug (bunched up
again) signalled someone familiar
with disorder. I stood hearing
a knot of wind undo at the window,
loose folds pouring down as you faded
through multiple scrims of the visible.

ALTERNATIVE FINGERING

Months, now, and you persist,
until you seem no more bizarre
than the ordinary, the arranged way
of things we know can break apart
like the earth at any minute if
the Big One comes or another
war begins or too much rain
makes the hill tear away
from itself as memory tears
away from my old mother's
brain. *My other*, I typed,
as if your once-upon-a-time
hand pressed down on mine,
boneless yet particulate, lifting
my finger just as it neared the *m*,
holding it suspended, symbol
of the body we have so much
less of day after day.

LUMINOUS ENVELOPE

So what am I to learn from you?
You do not know the names
of California wildflowers or birds.
You must have forgotten all
but the most basic stitches.
You remember how much dark
there is to endure, how the boat
and river are myth, how the only
passage is through the body,
the strange code spiralling down
through time and space, enclosed
in skin, luminous envelope you
would give anything to have again.
Live in mine, then. Keep being
with me. Feed on the reliable air.

The Power of the Great

She believes all things go on forever,
turn to darkness and dust and then rush back
remade – how a white dwarf
circles the Dog Star, howling in the night sky.

Lightning bugs, the luminescent bulbs
of their bellies flickering, live on and on,
their curious orbit turned to some
new form, then that too transfigured.

In spiderwebs she finds patterns of symmetry,
ley lines through the notch in a leaf,
the seven spokes and nine doorways
to a higher order.

Shapes and murmurs lurk in the bulging
blackness of space, wait for one more chance
to snap on the paired membrane
of wings and do good works.

She reads the Book of the Fixed Stars,
sets down her longings in the Book of Sorrow.
Far off she can hear the slow sigh
as stars travel over the lip

of the milky falls to flow into the arms
of Andromeda. One hour right ascension
to the northern sky. The eight bones
of her wrist lift, spill stardust from fingertips.

the tale the shepherds tell the sheep

that some will rise
above shorn clouds of fleece
and some will feel their bodies break
but most will pass through this
into sweet clover
where all all will be sheltered safe
until the holy shearing
don't think about the days to come
sweet meat
think of my arms
trust me

hold still my lives

I measure the ripening distance
        and the land falls away
        the expanses collecting like sorrows

the past also falls into bloom
        and I keep it gently, so close
        distance is what breaks it
        for it is like a sponge:
        brittle, an infinite hollow
        as meshed and absorbed
        as I, forever seeking
        a drop of animation –
        invitation into the world of
        unstuck things

and today comes with baby steps,
        unsure, the spaces in-between
        leaving infinity to grow
        and I both tend it
        and fear it
        for it is in constant increase
        like a fire fueled
        on the landscape of moments
        that like I, leaves all that the day builds
        abolished

for tomorrow is an ever-advancing not
        and I'm
        not ready   at all   for it

hold still my lives
        I'm trying to live you

The winner of the $1000 RUNES Award 2003

In a competition where the final judging
was done by poet Li-Young Lee.

MARK CHAPMAN of California
for his poem "Farming Below Sea Level"

The Runners Up were:
Lynne Knight of California for "Legacies"
Kyoko Uchida of the District of Columbia
for "Debt of Gratitude"

"It's not just language we use to write poems. We use silence, too.
In fact, I think we use language to inflect silence so we can hear it better."
–Li-Young Lee

The *2003 RUNES* **Award** poems, we think, are wonderful examples of what
Li-Young Lee means about using both language and silence. Like Li-Young Lee,
we were delighted with the quality of the poems submitted for the competition!

An Open Letter to Our Colleagues:

Over and over, the question arises: What do you have to do to get a poem into **RUNES**? This year we received over 7000 poems. The poems entered in our competition were read as part of the competition, then considered separately for possible publication. Of the 100 poems published here, 85 are by poets we've never published before. (Twelve contributors to **RUNES** 2002 came up to our table at the AWP Bookfair in Baltimore to meet us for the first time.) So what *are* we looking for? We're looking for spark and dazzle on the page, something risky, surprising, a poem that tells us something we don't already know. We have a taste for eccentricity (check out "Werewolf Lemonade" or "Cirque du Liz and Dick").

We read many of your submissions aloud looking for the music of the word, for a simple yet elegant mode of expression. In some way, we have to fall in love with each of the poems that makes it into **RUNES**. As narrative poets, we still like a poem that tells some kind of story; but we are eager to read and publish a wide variety of poetic styles. There simply isn't a single "RUNES type" poem.

So then, what *don't* we like. Some poems we received really seemed to be pieces of prose laid out like poetry. There were poems with too many ordinary adjectives or with too many weighty nouns like "soul," "heart," "bone," and "spirit." And, yes, we selected poems with these words. We even *write* poems that use them; but we're looking for poems that include them with subtlety and a kind of grace. Our deliberation process, which starts at our deadline of May 31st, takes 2 months – not really a long time but long enough that this year we "lost" four poems we really wanted to other publications that accepted them while we were still weighing our options.

We receive many 3, 4, even 5 page poems. We publish a number of them; but some of the long ones we receive sag and lose momentum in the middle. We also publish very short poems; but if a poem is short, it must pack a lot into a small space. One of us does not particularly like poems where the first person narrator uses a lower case "i;" yet we accepted a couple of those, too. Lastly, we received hundreds of very accomplished poems, ones sure to be snapped up elsewhere; and we were stunned at how hard it was to turn down them down.

Equally difficult (much more difficult than we ever imagined) was the process of saying no to friends, to editors who've published our work, and to well-known poets whose poems did not quite fit into the current issue.

Our aim is to treat you all with consideration and respect. We are trying to make your worlds and the world of poetry a little richer and more diverse. Our theme for 2004 will be "Storm" – literal storms and figurative ones. This letter is to those we've accepted, not accepted, and to all first-time submitters. Try us again. We look forward to reading your work.

'Lyn & Susan

RUNES Award 2004

RUNES, A Review of Poetry will be sponsoring
its third poetry competition in the spring of 2004.

The **RUNES Award 2004** will offer a $1000 prize plus publication in
RUNES, A Review of Poetry for an original, unpublished poem of 100
lines or less on the theme of "Storm." We are interested in metaphorical as
well as literal storms.

- There is an entry fee of $15 for 3 poems. The entry fee covers a one-
  year subscription to RUNES. Additional poems are $3 each.
- Your name should not appear on any of these poems.
- Each competition entry should include an SASE
  plus an 8" by 11" page with name, address, phone number, e-mail
  and title of each poem.

The final judge for this competition will be **Jane Hirshfield**.

Deadline: Submit only in April & May of 2004

All poems entered in the competition will be considered for publication in
the 2004 anthology.

It is **NOT** *necessary to enter the competition to have your poems considered for*
RUNES, *nor does entering the competition give any poet a better chance to have a*
poem accepted for publication.

All who wish to submit poems without entering the competition are
encouraged to do so. As in prior years, each poem will be read and assessed
on its own merit.

The theme for the 2004 issue will be "Storm," the same as the competition.

Submit only in April & May of 2004.

For additional information contact us at **RunesRev@aol.com**
or check our web site: **http://members.aol.com/Runes**

Send all competition entries and all submissions to:

RUNES, A Review of Poetry
Arctos Press, P.O. Box 401, Sausalito, CA 94966-0401

To our Subscribers:

We'd like to thank all of you for the faith and commitment you've offered. We have no university or parent organization funding us – only you. You have helped us out, shown us that interest in independent publishing is still alive.

For our other readers, if you're not already a subscriber, we hope you will consider becoming one. Perhaps you'll even want to send a gift subscription to friends or family members who have an interest in poetry. Maybe you'll take a copy of **RUNES** to your local bookstore and ask them to order it, or you'll consider subscribing for your local library. A year's subscription is only $12 and since **RUNES** is over 160 pages, that's only about 7 cents a page – a bargain in these expensive times.

To Submit:

Our reading period is April and May only of each year, so we will begin reading for "Storm" in April of 2004. This theme will be considered metaphorically as well as literally. Reports in four months. Acquires first time rights only.

We will consider simultaneous submissions, but please notify us promptly if a poem is accepted elsewhere. We do not accept previously published poems.

Send up to five poems with a **self-addressed stamped envelope** to:

RUNES, A Review of Poetry
Arctos Press, P.O, Box 401, Sausalito, CA 94966-0401

Do not send your only copies. Poems will be recycled, and handwritten poems will not be accepted. The e-mail is for correspondence only. Please do not submit via e-mail. Please remember the **SASE**. For additional information about submitting and for information about our annual competition **The RUNES Award**, check out our web site at: **http://members.aol.com/Runes**

All contributors will receive a copy of **RUNES** *'04 and have the opportunity to purchase additional copies at a discount.*

Subscription $12   Single copy $12   Sample Copy $10
2 year subscription $21